N. PAUL FRIEDERICHS

Beyond The Toxic Dance

Deepest Truths for Healing, Growth, and Lasting Transformation

First published by Banquet Table Press 2026

www.BeyondTheToxicDance.com

First edition

ISBN: 979-8-9996745-1-7

This book was professionally typeset on Reedsy.
Find out more at reedsy.com

To the One who heals what no one else can—
the Author of restoration, wisdom, and love.

This book is offered in quiet gratitude
for unseen guidance, enduring grace,
and the Presence who walks with us
when the way is long and the night is dark.

There is a path through pain—
not around it.

And when we walk it in truth,
we never walk alone.

Contents

Preface

Author's Note

Transformation has been at the heart of my journey. I've faced trauma less than some, more than others, and the process of survival and growth has shaped every part of me. I'm not ashamed of my story. In fact, I see it as something to celebrate. My circumstances weren't of my choosing; they chose me, just as circumstances often choose all of us. But my ongoing adventure has led to insights I believe can help others. Whether you're facing a specific struggle, trying to deepen a good relationship, or simply seeking to better understand yourself, you are welcome here.

Along this journey, I discovered something powerful: the Bible speaks profoundly to what we now call narcissism, empathy, and the hidden dynamics of relationships, and it changed everything for me. I also saw how psychology names and tests what Scripture has long revealed. Together, they create a fuller, clearer picture of the human heart than either can offer alone.

This book is complex, but so is the human experience. I didn't always see the world as I do now, and my needs have changed over time, just like yours have. Our views often balance different ideas and perspectives, shifting as we grow. By weaving four distinct perspectives, rather than narrowing the book to just one, it allows all of us to bring our views together in a way that feels more natural and far more respectful than what's typically found in a single voice or discipline.

That's why this book may feel like something different to each person who reads it.

If you are carrying trauma, it will feel like a recovery book offering insight, practical tools, and hope grounded in both research and timeless truth.

If you are skeptical of faith, it will feel like a conversation where psychological insight sheds light on enduring spiritual wisdom.

If you are a believer longing for more, it will feel like a spiritual road map, showing how God's Word and honest self-reflection lead to His heart.

You and another reader might sit side by side reading the same chapter, yet take away something very different. A trauma survivor might see the story of protection and resilience that helps them feel less alone. A skeptic might notice the psychological patterns confirmed by Scripture. A believer might see how those same psychological patterns were described in Scripture thousands of years ago. And yet the same core truth would quietly bind all three together.

How can one book speak to so many at once?

Because it's built on a single narrative arc: the journey from brokenness to wholeness. That arc has a shape: confusion gives way to clarity, pain yields to freedom, fractured relationships are restored to deeper love. It is told through four threads: personal narrative, trauma stories, psychology, and Scripture. Each reader naturally gravitates toward the thread that feels most urgent or familiar, while the others expand understanding, deepen empathy, and create a shared language that connects you with those who approach this journey differently.

You may wonder why I draw on both psychology and Scripture when so many believe only one is valid.

For believers, the Bible clearly calls us to "test everything; hold fast what is good" (1 Thessalonians 5:21). Psychology, at its best, tests human behavior and patterns. When its insights align with God's Word, they confirm and illuminate the truth already revealed. When they don't, they invite us to hold Scripture as the higher standard and gain discernment foretelling of the growth of psychology.

For those who trust only in science, ethical practice requires considering all credible sources of wisdom. Scripture has long been recognized even by secular scholars as a profound record of human motivations, resilience, failings, and relational dynamics. To dismiss it outright is not objective science; it is selective interpretation.

This book doesn't pit one against the other. It shows how the truth of Scripture and the best of human understanding can work together, revealing what the heart most deeply needs: safety, freedom, love, and transformation.

I am not an expert with lofty credentials. I'm a fellow traveler. What I bring comes from lived experience, not ivory towers. I don't claim to have all the answers, but I do offer what I've learned with honesty and hope.

Because you might see yourself in very different ways, let me speak directly to where you might be standing right now.

To Non-Believers

I respect your views and want you to know I'm not here to push or belittle. You have every right to believe as you choose. This book invites real, open conversation where psychology and Scripture are treated with equal respect. What if exploring both perspectives, psychological and spiritual, could open new pathways you haven't yet considered? You will be invited, but the choice of what you embrace as truth will always remain yours, affirmed even in the Epilogue.

To Believers

I, too, believe in Jesus Christ as my Lord and Savior. But this book isn't about reinforcing what we already know; it's about transformation. Be prepared to see the Bible in a new light, as God reveals His wisdom through lenses you may not have expected.

To Those Who Know They Have a Problem

I see you. I've been there too. You will understand this in Chapter 2 and elsewhere throughout the book. The pain you feel isn't weakness; it's your knowledge there is more, and your motivation to find it. Together, we'll uncover the patterns that once protected you, but now keep you stuck.

To Those With Narcissistic Traits

You are not invisible, nor are you beyond hope. I see you as a child of God, made in His image, longing for connection you've never fully known. This book will help those around you understand, empathize, and love you more easily, and it will empower you, while staying safe, to more easily be loved.

To Empaths

I know your heart, because this is me too. I know the exhaustion of always giving without feeling seen. Here, you'll find a way to love without losing yourself, to preserve the beautiful love you give, while staying safe and secure.

To Those Who Feel Everything Is Fine

Is it really? Or have you simply gotten used to the weight of life? Growth isn't only for the broken. It's for anyone who wants more. Enjoy an abundance of love without compromising personal safety in relationships.

No matter which of these describes you, or if you find pieces of yourself in all of them, you are part of this journey. And that is the beauty of it: we can walk this same road together even from very different starting points.

So let's honestly examine the tools psychology offers and see how they measure up to grace, forgiveness, and love. Our shared goal is the same: stronger, healthier relationships, rooted in safety, truth, and love.

Will you join me on this journey?

Let's step forward together toward healing, freedom, and a life transformed by grace.

With hope and anticipation,

N. Paul Friederichs

Introduction

The Narrow Path System: A Way to the Fullness and Completeness of Love and Security

We all begin in the same place with a deep need for love and security. And we all share the same destination: a life where both can exist together, uncompromised, in freedom.

But the road between those two points is rarely straight. While our individual paths are unique, we tend to take similar detours, getting lost, stuck, or unsure of the next step.

The Narrow Path System is more than a map connecting the beginning to the end. It shows where those detours are most likely to appear and how to find your way back. It offers a way forward into a life where love and security no longer have to compete.

As children, we often see life through a binary lens—either love or security. But in truth, there are four possible choices: love, security, neither, or both. That last one, both, is the destination. It's the fullness we long for, even if we don't always know how to get there.

The strategies we chose in childhood helped us survive, but over time they quietly harden into patterns that wound us or those we love. Some of us learned to disappear, minimizing our needs, walking on eggshells, or trying to earn love by staying small and agreeable. Others, afraid of being unseen, reached for control, applause, or perfection to feel secure. Whether your instinct was to keep the peace or take the lead, the goal was the same: safety.

But safety without connection becomes its own kind of prison. The result is often disconnection, confusion, or invisible wounds that echo through adult relationships.

As Jesus said in Matthew 7:14, "But small is the gate and narrow the road that leads to life, and only a few find it." (NIV). The Narrow Path System was designed to help you find it, not by striving harder, but by understanding the map.

If you're skeptical or unsure about faith, or even if you're simply curious, this path is still for you. The journey doesn't require you to have all the answers up front, only an open heart and a willingness to explore. Whether you approach it as spiritual wisdom, practical guidance, or a framework for emotional healing, the goal is the same: to step into a life where love and security are no longer distant or elusive.

You'll also find a summary of the deeper shifts woven through this journey, what I call foundational disruptions, in Appendix C. They're not an afterthought; they're the hidden framework behind every chapter. These disruptions gently rewire how we think, feel, relate, and heal.

No matter where you start, you're invited to explore, ask questions, and walk this path at your own pace.

This book is for everyone—whether you've lost your way or are simply searching for a better path to healing and growth. Maybe everything in your life feels wonderful. If so, do you truly understand why others are struggling? You interact with them. You care about them. And loving them well means understanding them better.

Or maybe you're more like me—someone who had to make painful choices before discovering a different way. I'll share some of those with you.

Wherever you find yourself, this is your invitation to rediscover freedom—not just emotionally, but in the deep places where your heart still hopes for peace, connection, and wholeness—spiritually and relationally.

Welcome to *Beyond the Toxic Dance*. Let's walk the Narrow Path together.

1

Part 1: What Gets in the Way of Love

Coping vs. Transformation

You were born dancing.

But whose music have you been moving to? And how much of it was never truly yours?

Before you even heard the rhythm of your own heart, your feet were already following steps you didn't choose. Many of us stay in that dance for years, worn out, silent, surviving instead of thriving before we ever stop to ask why our relationships feel dull, strained, or painful. We learned those steps early: how to avoid conflict, stay needed, and keep the peace. We didn't choose the choreography. We inherited it.

And what we inherited helped us survive.

In a world that prizes hustle and achievement, many confuse busyness and performance for love. We chase approval, measure worth by success, and forget that true connection requires more than just showing up. This cultural noise can drown out the quiet voice inside, the part of you that longs for real belonging and freedom.

Part 1 honors that truth while asking a deeper question: Are the strategies that once kept you safe still aligned with love, healing, and truth? Here, we'll explore what gets in the way of love—not just love as a fleeting feeling, but something more foundational: attachment, honesty, safety, grace, and transformation. Psychology shines a light on the behaviors we fall into: people-pleasing, perfectionism, avoidance, control while Scripture reveals the soul's deeper wounds and points toward lasting healing. Together, these perspectives don't merely expose what's broken. They invite a powerful union showing how science and faith together can move us beyond coping and into true transformation.

You won't be asked to reject your old strategies. Instead, you'll be invited to notice when the very patterns that once protected you are now holding you back.

This book isn't about fixing what's broken in you. It's about freeing what's truest in you—what fear tried to bury but never destroyed. We will gently remove a costume you only thought was you.

The agreements that once shielded us, but now chain us, will come into the light. We'll begin to lift the masks we perfected—the false selves that stole our freedom and our truth. In the words of Scripture, we are being transformed with unveiled faces (2 Corinthians 3:18, NIV), not by force, but by grace, as we return to who we were always meant to be.

Your coping carried you through the storm, and that's no small thing. But now the path narrows, calling you from survival into the fullness of freedom, love, and unshakable truth.

As you begin this journey, here's a simple tool to carry with you:

For one week, notice when you feel most like your true self, and when you feel like you're wearing a mask. Pay attention to the moments when you feel relaxed, open, and clear. Then notice when you feel hidden, smaller, or like you're managing others' expectations. You might journal once a day or simply pause for thirty seconds after a hard moment.

There's no need to fix anything yet. Just pay attention. Awareness itself is part of the healing.

Let's begin by tracing the hidden roots so we can stop performing love and start living it, rooted in a truth that doesn't just inform you but transforms you.

You were born dancing. Now it's time to choose the music that moves your soul.

Sometimes, that music feels beautiful. Sometimes, it pulls you into places you never intended to go.

2

Chapter 1: Hidden Roots of Relationship Struggles

Jason didn't see it coming.

At first, Sheila seemed like the kind of person everyone hopes to meet at a new job, warm, funny, instantly welcoming. Their friendship formed fast. But then something shifted. Her warmth gave way to sharp comments. Her support became pressure. One day, he was her trusted friend; the next, he was walking on eggshells. Jason felt confused, exhausted, and unsure if the connection had ever been real.

What went wrong?

What Jason experienced wasn't just miscommunication. It was the fallout of a deeper imbalance, the quiet conflict between two essential needs: connection and protection.

This isn't just Jason's story. It's the story behind countless relationships. And if you've ever given your best to someone only to feel more lost, this chapter is for you.

Maybe you've asked yourself, "Why do I keep ending up in relationships where I give more than I get?" That question is more common and more revealing than it seems.

Most people search for answers in the symptoms: communication breakdowns, trust issues, toxic patterns. But those struggles don't appear out of nowhere. They grow from hidden roots, internal agreements we made long ago about love, safety, and worth.

Quick fixes may soothe the surface. But they can't heal what's buried deeper.

There's an ancient prayer that captures the courage it takes to look inward: "Search me, God, and know my heart; test me and know my anxious thoughts" (Psalm 139:23–24, NIV).

Whether you read it as poetry, faith, or simply wisdom passed down, the invitation is the same: transformation begins when we dare to look beneath the surface.

At our core, two fundamental needs shape us: love and security. When those needs are out of balance, we suffer. Some of us prioritize security and build walls. Others cling to love and sacrifice themselves to preserve it. Most of us shift between the two, depending on the situation.

These patterns aren't signs of failure. They're signposts pointing us toward a better way. A way that doesn't require choosing between love and safety.

That's what this chapter is about.

We're going to look deeper past the symptoms, past the strategies, to the hidden roots that shape how we relate. You'll see how early needs drive adult choices, how comfort can become a substitute for connection, and how sacrificial love, when unbalanced, can quietly lead to self-neglect.

These aren't just psychological insights. They're invitations to heal, to grow, and to experience a kind of love that doesn't just feel safe, but sets you free.

I invite you to walk that path with me.

Why Simple Solutions Fall Short

Many people, in their search for relief, lean on quick fixes. Popular self-help strategies promise comfort but tend to focus on managing symptoms rather than addressing the root cause of pain. Breathing exercises, mindfulness techniques, or simple counting methods may soothe the moment, but they rarely transform the source of the struggle.

It's like treating a deep infection with painkillers—silencing the alarm while the disease quietly spreads, unseen and unchecked. The pain may subside, but the infection festers beneath the surface. True healing begins when we go beneath the symptoms to address the underlying cause.

You may have learned very early how to cope with the challenges in your relationships. From a tender age, you likely mastered coping as a survival dance—a necessary shield that, over time, became a cage.

Perhaps you perfected the art of smiling through chaos, keeping everything running amid dysfunction. Maybe you shut down emotionally when things got tough, avoiding conflict or sacrificing your needs to keep the peace. Or you may have taken a more authoritative stance, trying to control your environment to feel safe.

Even with these strategies, a sense of emptiness can linger. If things truly felt right inside, you wouldn't keep repeating the same unhealthy patterns or feel stuck in cycles that wear you down.

While psychology shines light on the behaviors we fall into, it often leaves the soul's deeper needs in shadow—those longings that only grace and truth can reach. Many popular psychology approaches help us adapt, teaching us ways to manage anxiety or reframe thoughts. These tools can be valuable, especially in moments of crisis. But often, they stop short of uncovering the deep wounds beneath the surface—the places where fear, shame, or abandonment have taken root in the soul.

Without addressing those, relief is temporary, and the pain waits for its next chance to resurface.

At the same time, many mainstream solutions overlook the spiritual and moral dimensions of healing. They treat symptoms as isolated problems, ignoring how beliefs, unresolved hurts, and life narratives shape our relational patterns. Healing at this level requires more than changing behaviors—it calls for a transformation of mind, heart, and soul.

Alice and Friends: A Fictional Story

Alice had learned early to keep her heart safe by building high walls around herself. She convinced herself that if she didn't need anyone, she wouldn't be vulnerable to pain.

Her walls were strong—too strong for anyone to get through. She appeared steady and self-reliant, but inside, a profound loneliness echoed through rooms she kept locked tight. She longed for connection but didn't know how to trust again.

One evening, a close friend gently confronted her:

"You push people away, Alice. You don't let anyone in."

At first, Alice felt defensive and scared. Yet as she reflected, the truth sank in. Her walls had protected her from pain, but also imprisoned her in isolation.

Choosing to lower those walls was terrifying; each brick loosened felt like stepping off a cliff into the unknown, where the safety of solitude gave way to the risk of heartbreak. But Alice also discovered something she had forgotten: vulnerability is the gateway to real connection.

She started taking small steps toward opening her heart, learning that true safety isn't found in walls but in honest relationships. Over time, those walls crumbled, and she found a depth of connection that survived imperfection and pain.

Alice's journey illustrates a vital truth: coping has its place, but it is only the first step. True transformation begins when we recognize and release old patterns that no longer serve us.

It requires courage to face the fear beneath the defense, to let go of control, and to invite grace and honesty into our relationships. Transformation is not a comfortable retreat from pain, but a courageous journey through it, a rising toward the fullness and freedom we were always meant to inhabit.

As Scripture invites us with gentle yet unyielding clarity: "Do not conform to the pattern of this world, but be transformed by the renewing of your mind" (Romans 12:2, NIV).

This call transcends religious boundaries. Even if faith feels distant or unfamiliar, the invitation is clear: choose to exchange automatic, fearful reactions for conscious, life-giving choices, choices that free you to love and be loved without fear.

When love and security are tended together—root and branch—we begin to bear fruit that nourishes not only ourselves but the world around us.

This transformation leads to a wholeness that coping cannot provide. It frees us from the exhausting dance of survival, the silent bargains we make in fear, and the masks we wear to hide our true selves. It opens us to the peace, joy, and relational health we all crave.

Reflection Question

Pause for a moment. What recurring patterns color your relationships? Which beliefs or habits whisper for release—yearning for transformation that leads you to safety, love, and wholeness?

Final Thought

Rooted in truth and watered by grace, love grows strong enough to hold you. And in that place, you discover the wholeness you were always meant to carry.

How Early Needs Shape Our Adult Choices

According to Maslow's Hierarchy of Needs, love and security are as vital to the soul as air and water are to the body. Without them, a child may survive but cannot truly thrive.

Love tells us we matter. Security assures us we're safe. Both are essential. Neither should be compromised. When poured like concrete in childhood, they become the unseen base for every future relationship.

Research confirms what the soul already knows. Mid-20th-century studies of orphanages and hospitals found infants who received food and shelter but were deprived of emotional connection—no touch, no comfort, no love—often failed to thrive. Many stopped eating. Some even died. The absence of human warmth wasn't just sad. It was deadly.

This isn't only about babies. It's about all of us. The need for love and safety runs deeper than we often realize. Without them, something essential inside withers. With them, we grow—not just in body, but in spirit, trust, and joy.

Whatever your early experience—whether marked by consistency or chaos—you developed scripts in childhood that still influence you today. Some helped you thrive. Others were coping mechanisms that simply helped you survive. Either way, they became default patterns you now carry into adulthood.

For many, love felt conditional or unpredictable. So we learned to shape ourselves around others' expectations. We became performers. Achievers. Chameleons. If we got it right, maybe our world would feel right.

Others grew up in unsafe environments. We learned to track every mood, anticipate every need, and manage the instability around us. Not because we were flawed, but because we were smart. We adapted. That's what children do.

Even in nurturing homes, no childhood is perfect. We all picked up beliefs and behaviors that made sense then—but may no longer serve us now.

Psychologists call this attachment theory—the idea that early experiences of love and safety shape our emotional resilience. When those needs go unmet, we develop strategies to protect ourselves. Some cling tightly to relationships, terrified of abandonment. Others push people away, fearing they'll be hurt again. Neither is permanent. They're temporary responses to pain—but eventually, we're invited to grow beyond them.

Attachment theory names the pattern. Scripture names the person—the beloved child of God, shaped by wounds but not defined by them.

Maybe you spent years putting everyone else first, anticipating needs, diffusing tension, smiling through it all. That wasn't weakness. It was a strategy—a brilliant child trying to earn love through self-sacrifice.

Or maybe you went the other way. You closed off, built walls, and carried the weight alone. That, too, was protection—another path to feeling safe.

And all of it made sense then. Proverbs 22:6 (NIV) says, "Start children off on the way they should go, and even when they are old, they will not turn from it." Our early paths shape us, but they don't have to define us forever. With awareness, we can begin to choose something new.

Beneath both people-pleasing and controlling behaviors lies the same deep human longing: connection and protection. These aren't character flaws. They're learned responses—understandable, human, deeply relational.

But those responses come with consequences. They shape how we relate, what we fear, and what we tolerate. And when relationships feel stuck or strained, it's often because those old strategies are still running the show.

This is where practical change begins—seeing the old patterns clearly and moving beyond them. When we can name the pattern without shame, we can choose differently.

That's why we look back—not to dwell, but to understand. When we trace the roots of our habits, we stop blaming ourselves or others. We begin to see clearly. And that clarity is the start of change.

Let's do that together.

A Journey of Transformation: A Personal Story

Like you, I've had relationships that left lasting marks, some painful, others life-giving. You'll hear more of my story throughout this book, but for now, here's what I want you to know:

I'm one of the foster kids who made it.

I didn't just survive. I learned to build a life from broken pieces. I became a student of pain, a translator of hard-won truths, and a witness to the surprising power of grace. My scars became maps.

And while I don't hold a psychology degree or counseling license, I've gained something equally powerful: real-life wisdom. I've walked through struggle, wrestled with pain, and explored healing through psychology, counseling, and Scripture. Then something clicked. Freedom became real.

I transformed. And I'm here to tell you, "You can, too."

This book is a road map, one I traveled myself and now offer to you. Along the way, I found tools that helped me break free from cycles of pain, rebuild my self-worth, and experience peace. These lessons apply to anyone who wants to grow. Whether you're beginning recovery or refining what's already strong, these aren't theories. They're truths that worked for me and for others I've helped along the way.

When I finished writing this book, I paused to reflect. Should I keep this experience private? After all, I don't have traditional credentials.

But then I remembered Moses, David, and others who felt underqualified. Yet God used them powerfully.

I also thought about how many breakthroughs in history came from outsiders. The LCD watch, for example, wasn't invented by the Swiss, despite their dominance in watchmaking. It came from a small team in Japan who saw things differently.

Sometimes the best answers come from people who refuse to give up, even when they don't fit the mold.

So I chose to share this not because I have all the answers, but because I've lived the questions and found a way forward. It worked for me. It's worked for others. And it can work for you.

Narcissist and Empath: A Shared Reflection

Think of empathic and narcissistic behaviors like handedness. Most of us have a dominant hand, but we still use the other. These traits exist on a spectrum. Very few people live entirely at one end. Only a small percentage meet the criteria for Narcissistic Personality Disorder (NPD), but many exhibit narcissistic patterns. Likewise, most people express empathy just not in every relationship or situation.

This idea of handedness is why I'm writing this book the way I am. I won't demonize narcissistic people, as many books do, because in truth, that's all of us. I won't place empaths on a pedestal, because that, too, is all of us. Instead, we'll closely examine these styles to help light the path toward relationship patterns that actually free us.

Reflection Question

Think back to your childhood. How did the need for love and security shape the way you engage in relationships today? Are there patterns you recognize that started long ago?

This week, choose one situation where an old pattern shows up. Pause for 30 seconds and ask yourself: What am I trying to protect right now—love, safety, or both? Then take one small action that reflects the person you're becoming, not just who you had to be.

Final Thought

Love and safety are not optional. You need both without compromise. As you continue, let that truth settle deeper than the fear that once shaped you. There is a better way forward, and you've already stepped onto it—one foot in grace, the other in courage.

Self-Protection and the Loss of Love

We all begin in the same place with a deep need for both love and security. But somewhere along the way, some of us start choosing comfort over connection, mistaking protection for peace.

It's understandable. Comfort feels safe. It shields us from risk, disappointment, and pain. But when comfort becomes our highest goal, it quietly costs us the very thing our hearts long for most: meaningful connection.

In today's world, success often masquerades as security—wealth, predictability, control. None of these are bad in themselves. But when they become the shelter we hide behind, we protect ourselves so well that no one can truly reach us. We build cold fortresses to feel safe, only to discover we're the ones locked inside.

From a psychological standpoint, this kind of self-protection often grows from unresolved relational wounds, moments when vulnerability led to pain instead of safety. When early risks brought rejection or chaos, the nervous system learned to associate closeness with danger. Over time, distance became the default—not because it's what we wanted, but because it's what once kept us safe.

Self-protection can look like many things: avoiding difficult conversations, building walls of busyness, or numbing feelings with distractions. Sometimes it's a quiet whisper inside that insists, "I'm better off alone." These subtle habits accumulate over time, shaping a life that feels safe on the surface but hollow underneath.

Remember the patterns we explored in the last section—the scripts learned from childhood that told us how to stay safe? Self-protection is often those scripts running on autopilot, telling us to keep our distance and avoid risk. But while those strategies once served us, they can also keep us trapped in isolation.

Scripture speaks to this very tension: "Pride goes before destruction, a haughty spirit before a fall" (Proverbs 16:18, NIV). Pride doesn't always shout. Sometimes it whispers, "I'm fine on my own. I don't need anyone." But self-protection disguised as strength can quietly become our identity, isolating us from the love and belonging we were made for.

And that isolation doesn't always feel like loneliness. Sometimes, it feels like resentment. Or control. Or unforgiveness. We hold on to pain because releasing it feels like surrendering power. But here's the truth: what feels like protection can become a snare.

Forgiveness is not pretending the pain didn't matter. It's choosing not to let it chain you. It's an essential step back toward connection. We'll explore forgiveness more deeply later, but for now, know this: without it, love cannot fully grow. And where love can't grow, security becomes an illusion.

If you're wondering where to begin, start by noticing. What do you guard most in your relationships? What feels too risky to share? You don't have to force vulnerability overnight, but naming your patterns without judgment is powerful. Awareness opens space for something new and prepares your heart for the forgiveness and connection ahead.

We weren't meant to do life alone. "Two are better than one. If either of them falls down, one can help the other up" (Ecclesiastes 4:9–10, NIV). We are stronger, safer, and more fully alive when we allow ourselves to be known. Vulnerability may feel risky, but it's the only soil where true connection can take root.

Success Without Connection: A Fictional Story

Michael had everything his peers admired: a respected career, financial stability, and a polished life. But beneath the surface, there was an ache he couldn't name. His relationships were distant. His laughter felt scripted. He had spent years perfecting an image until the cost became impossible to ignore.

At a high school reunion, something unexpected happened. For the first time in years, Michael stopped performing. He listened. Old friends spoke of regrets and reconciliations, of loss and healing. Their honesty unsettled him—and awakened something. Their stories gave him permission to feel his own.

That night, Michael let his guard down just a little. He shared something real. And in that small risk, something shifted. He felt seen for who he truly was.

Change didn't come all at once. But the door opened. Michael began to reach out more, to let people in. As the walls lowered, he found something surprising: he felt stronger and more alive. Less alone. More whole.

His story isn't rare. It's a reminder that comfort may keep us safe, but it's connection that makes us human.

Reflection Question

Some people instinctively prioritize safety, stability, or comfort. Others lean toward openness, connection, and emotional closeness. Which do you naturally value more—and in which areas of your life?

As you journal, name the fears that arise: fear of aloneness, fear of harm, fear of loss. Simply naming these fears brings them into truthful awareness, softening their grip.

Final Thought

What looks like peace isn't always peace. Sometimes, it's just control in disguise. But the deeper invitation is still open: you don't have to choose between love and safety.

The Dangers of Self-Neglect

As an empath, choosing love over security can seem noble—sometimes even heroic. You might pour yourself into others, go the extra mile, or carry the weight of someone else's comfort on your shoulders. But beneath this quiet sacrifice lies a hidden cost: your own safety and dignity.

Many of us learned early that being good meant not rocking the boat. We became skilled at smoothing things over, meeting expectations, and staying agreeable to preserve connection. Over time, these strategies became second nature. We gave love freely, even sacrificially, but held our breath when it came to asking for the same in return.

In relationships, this kind of imbalance can look like devotion. In reality, it often reflects fear—the fear that if we stop giving, others may stop loving us. That fear quietly erodes the boundaries that protect our heart and spirit.

A dangerous pattern forms: the more uncertain the relationship feels, the more we over-function to hold the crumbling pieces together. The more we feel unseen, the more we shrink. We become so focused on meeting someone else's needs that we forget we have needs of our own. Yet Scripture gently reminds us: "You shall have no other gods before me" (Exodus 20:3, NIV).

Love that asks us to disappear isn't love. It's a slow erosion of the self.

Even Jesus—who modeled the deepest expression of love—never lost His sense of self. He said no. He walked away. He took time to rest. His passion was not rooted in appeasement; it was rooted in truth.

Scripture helps us recalibrate our understanding of love: "Do not use your freedom to indulge the flesh; rather, serve one another humbly in love" (Galatians 5:13, NIV). Notice the balance—freedom, service, humility, and love. True love honors both people in the relationship. It doesn't ask one to vanish so the other can thrive.

Healing begins when we honor the sacred balance between vulnerability and strength. It invites us to embrace our limits without shame and to offer ourselves compassion when we fall short. This is the kind of love that transforms—not by erasing us, but by restoring us. It's the difference between self-sacrifice that destroys and self-love that renews.

Schooling: A Personal Story

Growing up with a father driven by recognition and a mother afraid to step into his place, I experienced neglect. That void shaped my hunger for attention. I believed that if I just gave more, I could prove I was worthy.

That mindset followed me into law school. I worked full time while attending an accelerated three-year program—a pace nearly unheard of. Those working full time typically followed a four-year track. But I was determined to excel. Somehow, I also won three moot court competitions and represented my school at nationals.

I needed to complete the coursework faster than it could even be credited. Some of my grades were floating credits, appearing on my transcript only after graduation. On paper, I walked with my class. In reality, I had been sprinting the entire time.

I wasn't living. I was surviving. I was so consumed with proving my worth that I lost sight of everything else. I sacrificed sleep, health, and connection. I believed success would satisfy the ache I carried. Instead, I ended up depleted, anxious, and profoundly alone.

I was watering every garden but my own, wondering why I felt so dry.

Eventually, I hit bottom and came face to face with a truth I couldn't ignore: self-neglect is the silent thief of joy.

What I truly sought was to be seen and valued. But what I found was a cycle of exhaustion and self-abandonment. That moment became a turning point.

Our stories may differ, but the ache beneath them—the desire to be seen and safe—is the same. We are all seeking a path that offers both love and security without compromising either. We may be in different places on this journey, but we walk a shared road. This book illuminates that narrow path toward healing.

Reflection Question

Have you ever felt like others took your kindness for granted or overlooked your needs in a relationship? How did that affect your sense of self-worth and the choices you made?

This week, schedule one 30-minute block of time for yourself with no productivity goals—just restoration. Read, walk, rest, create—whatever refreshes your soul. Water your own garden first.

Final Thought

Loving others, while vital, is not by itself a complete path to love and security. We need both—love that nourishes and boundaries that protect. Honoring your worth, setting wise limits, and extending grace are the pillars that lead to a more peaceful, authentic, and resilient life.

* * *

Even the most generous love must make room for the one who gives it. Let today be the day you stop bleeding to be seen and instead begin the journey to wholeness where your worth is recognized not by others, but by your own steadfast heart.

You've now seen the hidden roots: how early needs shape adult choices, how comfort can become a substitute for connection, and how even love itself can quietly twist into self-neglect. These patterns are not random. They're survival strategies—wise for a season, but costly over time.

The good news is this: what was learned can be unlearned. What was wounded can be healed. What once chained you can become a steppingstone to deeper freedom.

The first step was naming the patterns. The next is redefining what love really is.

Because love—real love—isn't just a feeling, an obligation, or a transaction. It's deeper. Stronger. More enduring than the counterfeits we've often mistaken for the real thing.

In Chapter 2, we'll ask the question, "What Is Love, Really?" We'll look at the language of love from the ancient past to today, and uncover the difference between shallow commitments that break us and the enduring power of Agape that heals us. We'll explore not just what love is, but how it frees us to live deeply and authentically moving beyond the worn scripts and into the heart of true connection.

3

Chapter 2: What Is Love Really?

You thought you knew what love was until it left you aching, confused, or afraid. Maybe it came wrapped in tenderness one moment and silence the next. Maybe it showed up as approval you had to earn, or promises that felt safe until they broke.

I've been there too—clinging to the love I knew, even when it left me empty and uncertain. We give love our all: trust, loyalty, even silence. We pour ourselves out, only to wonder why love so often feels unsafe—like sand slipping through our fingers.

Love is not what we feel in the moment but what we choose to hold onto when the moment passes. True love doesn't begin with attraction or approval; it begins with recognizing worth that cannot be lost.

Here's the hard truth: what we learned as love through culture, family, or experience can be incomplete. Sometimes it's not love at all—just fear in disguise. Sometimes it's obligation, or survival, or the only form of connection we were ever taught. We called it love because we didn't know there was more. But what if the way we've learned to love is missing not just depth, but direction? Not just feeling, but foundation?

The English language doesn't help us much. One word—love—is expected to carry the weight of our most casual preferences and our deepest bonds. We say we love our children, our favorite show, our best friend, our spouse and lasagna. The same word flattens wildly different experiences. It's a shortcut that costs us clarity.

And without clarity, love becomes something we chase without understanding, offer without boundaries, and try to earn without ever feeling secure.

This confusion quietly distorts our hearts. We begin to think love is a feeling that fades when things get hard, or a transaction that exists only if it's reciprocated. We give too much in the wrong places—or withhold what someone truly needs because we feel empty ourselves. We confuse affection with obligation, kindness with intimacy, and approval with value. And when those lines blur, our hearts get lost in the fog.

So let's clear the fog.

A Framework Shaped by the Past

Ancient Greek culture handled love with more care and nuance. They knew one word couldn't hold the full spectrum of human connection, so they used several. Each one carried a different meaning, shaped by intention, context, and proximity.

Naming those distinctions helped people recognize what kind of relationship they were in—and what boundaries were wise within it.

Take Eros, for instance, the word for romantic or passionate love. At its best, Eros involves mutual longing, emotional intimacy, and a desire to unite both physically and spiritually. But Eros without roots is volatile. When awakened prematurely or shared without clarity, it stirs expectations the relationship may not be strong enough to hold. What feels intoxicating at first can leave us empty, exposed, or entangled in something our soul can't sustain.

Then there's Philia, the love of friendship. It grows slowly, built through shared experience, mutual respect, and trust. Philia doesn't rush intimacy but invites connection over time. It gives us room to be ourselves, to be known and accepted. Jesus Himself told His disciples, "Greater love has no one than this: to lay down one's life for one's friends" (John 15:13, NIV). That's Philia, friendship that commits, shows up, and stays present.

Storge, another form of love, is the natural affection within families, between parents and children, or siblings. It feels instinctual but still needs nurturing. Left unchecked, it can grow possessive or conditional. Familiarity alone doesn't guarantee safety. Scripture warns gently: "Fathers, do not provoke your children to anger, but bring them up in the discipline and instruction of the Lord" (Ephesians 6:4, NIV). Healthy Storge blends tenderness with truth, protection with wisdom.

But what about the kind of love that doesn't fit easily into these categories? Love for strangers or even enemies? The Greeks didn't have a single word for that.

Jesus didn't just expand love beyond what was convenient. He shattered every category. "Love your enemies and pray for those who persecute you" (Matthew 5:44, NIV). This love doesn't require affection or agreement. It simply asks us to will the good of another—to see even the difficult person as someone worthy of dignity and compassion.

When we choose not to pass on the pain we've received, we break the cycle. We begin to shape a different culture—one where love isn't defined by likeness or convenience, but by commitment to something higher.

That brings us to Agape.

Agape is more than just another type of love. It's the thread that holds all true love together. Unlike the other forms, Agape isn't about closeness—it's about consistency. It's the choice to keep love at the center even when there's no affection, no agreement, no reciprocation. It's not sentiment. It's not softness. It's a fierce commitment to love as a way of being.

Agape reshapes us from the inside out. Not because it feels good, but because it changes everything.

A Quick Pause for You

Think of one relationship in your life that feels confusing. Is it marked by Eros, Philia, Storge—or something else? Does it hold Agape? Naming what kind of love is present might clarify what boundaries or expectations are healthy.

Now that we've named the many faces of love, we'll look at what holds these loves together—what it means to stay committed when feelings change or challenges arise.

Take a moment to consider how these different types of love have shaped your life, where they brought joy, and where they left questions unanswered.

Reflection Question

How might understanding the types of love help you set clearer, healthier boundaries?

This week, reflect on the kinds of love present in your relationships. When you feel overwhelmed, ask: What kind of love is this? Is it a transaction? What is its true foundation?

Final Thought

Love isn't one-size-fits-all. It's a language of care and commitment shaped by context, proximity, and truth. When we understand what love truly is—and what it is not—we gain the freedom to give it more wisely and receive it more securely. This clarity prepares us to name the imitations that have wounded us, which we'll explore next.

The Commitment Behind Love: Counterfeit vs. Agape

What does it really mean to stay committed to love?

When feelings shift, when disappointment creeps in, when someone frustrates or fails us, what does real love require?

That's where the difference between counterfeit love and Agape love becomes unmistakably clear.

Worth Noticing: A Fictional Story

When Vanessa's new boss arrived, he seemed like a dream. He praised her work in front of the team, brought her coffee just the way she liked it, and told her she reminded him of someone he deeply respected. Within days, lunch invitations and long personal chats became routine. He even hinted she was on the fast track for a promotion.

Vanessa found herself working harder, eager to please.

But then the tone shifted. One day, she disagreed with a small decision. The warmth cooled. Suddenly she was excluded from meetings, and subtle questions about her loyalty began circulating. The praise dried up.

A coworker quietly pulled her aside. "This isn't about you. He does this every time. It starts with charm; it ends with control."

It hit her all at once. That flood of attention wasn't love—or even mentorship. It was manipulation wrapped in flattery. The moment she stopped meeting his unspoken expectations, the love vanished.

Vanessa had been caught in classic love bombing—a rush of charm meant to gain influence, not connection. She learned to stop measuring praise as proof of love. Instead, she began leading with clarity, not compliance, and found peace again.

Counterfeit Love

Counterfeit love often looks real. It mimics affection, uses the language of devotion, and may even begin with good intentions. But underneath, it's fueled by fear, control, insecurity, or self-protection. It exploits our deepest need for love and safety, creating slavish devotion in the unwary.

Psychologically, counterfeit love is always conditional. It whispers, "I'll love you if…" or "I'll stay as long as…" It's transactional—rooted in how well someone meets the internal needs of the one offering love. Performance, obligation, or power quietly drive it. Love is given, but never freely. Strings are always attached.

Many of us learned these patterns early, earning love through achievement or compliance. We carried that belief into adulthood, turning relationships into proving grounds for our worth. Love became something to hustle for, not a place to rest.

The result? Love that feels intense but unstable. We become addicted to the highs of attention and terrified of the lows of disconnection. We shape ourselves to meet expectations just to keep others close. Or we withdraw love as punishment, using silence, distance, or guilt to control.

Worse still, counterfeit love wears the mask of sacrifice: "I give everything for you." But hidden beneath is the demand: "so you'll never leave."

Fear is always at the root—fear of abandonment, failure, or simply not being enough. And when fear is the foundation, the relationship cannot hold.

This pain might feel familiar. It's a common detour off the narrow path. But naming it is the first step toward freedom. We're not here to stay stuck in the hurt—we're here to see it clearly so we can leave it behind.

Agape Love

Agape love is entirely different. Worthiness, reciprocation, performance—they have no place here.

Agape is a willful, anchored choice to seek another's good. It is the only love that remains when everything else crumbles.

Humiliated and facing death, Jesus demonstrated this love with piercing clarity: "Father, forgive them, for they do not know what they are doing" (Luke 23:34, NIV). No apology. No confession. No sign of remorse. Yet love flowed anyway.

How would you respond after such humiliation of being whipped, nailed to a cross, and taunted?

Agape doesn't wait for someone to become lovable. It doesn't require agreement, perfection, or mutual affection. It's about how we choose to treat others—with honor, dignity, and compassion—even when it's hard.

But let's be clear: Agape isn't blind or passive. It doesn't tolerate abuse or excuse harm. Boundaries matter deeply. True Agape often demands strength—to confront, to say no, or to walk away from patterns that destroy. Love that permits destruction isn't love; it's complicity.

Agape protects, even if protection means distance. It holds firm in truth, even when truth costs.

As Scripture reminds us: "Love is patient, love is kind. It does not envy, it does not boast, it is not proud. It does not dishonor others, it is not self-seeking, it is not easily angered, it keeps no record of wrongs. Love does not delight in evil but rejoices with the truth. It always protects, always trusts, always hopes, always perseveres. Love never fails" (1 Corinthians 13:4–8a, NIV).

Sit with these words. They may feel foreign at first—especially if the love you've known lacked a firm foundation. But when the foundation is right, these words stop feeling impossible.

We'll explore that foundation next.

A Love We Grow Into

Agape isn't something we offer perfectly from the start. It's something we grow into as we heal.

When we name and release counterfeit patterns, space opens for something deeper. Agape becomes not only possible but natural.

Agape isn't rare because it's unreachable. It's rare because it requires courage. It demands clarity. Above all, it calls for commitment—to stand in the truth about ourselves and others, and love anyway. Honestly. Wisely. Without fear.

If counterfeit love is about control, Agape is about faithfulness to love itself. Whether in marriage, friendship, parenting, leadership, or even how we treat strangers and enemies, Agape is the anchor. It shapes who we are and how we move through the world.

Jesus didn't just tell us to love this way. He lived it. Now, He invites us to do the same.

Reflection Question

Where in my life am I offering love based on conditions or fear? What would it look like to shift toward love that protects, trusts, hopes, and perseveres?

Final Thought

Counterfeit love asks little of the giver but costs everyone involved.

Agape love demands something deeper: the courage to remain committed to love even when it stretches us. But in that stretch, we don't break—we grow.

And in growing, we learn not only to receive love more freely but to become the kind of people—without fear or compromise—who can finally give it.

What Truly Holds Love Together?

It may surprise us to admit that every form of love—even Agape—rests on a condition. The difference lies in what kind of condition holds that love in place. Some are shallow and brittle. Others are deep and enduring. Some collapse under pressure. Others stand steady through every storm.

When we say condition here, we're not just talking about requirements or rules, but the underlying reality that either supports or undermines love's endurance. What breaks love most often isn't the absence of affection, but the foundation beneath it.

Think of it this way: a love's condition is its foundation. Some are built on shifting sand; others rest on solid rock. What happens over time depends entirely on what lies beneath the surface.

Fleeting conditions often begin invisibly. They sound like affection or connection but hide a secret: they're built on need, approval, performance, or emotional exchange.

These are fragile conditions. Love fades when the condition isn't met. Warmth cools when performance slips. Affection withdraws when someone fails to give back just right. In those cases, the love was never really about the other person—it was about what they provided in return.

Many of us have felt the sting of love tied to physical attraction, social status, or emotional convenience. It's thrilling at first but vulnerable to the shifting winds of circumstance. This kind of love falters under stress, disappointment, or conflict. It breeds insecurity, leaving us anxious, watchful, scrambling to hold on.

Psychologists call these anxious or avoidant attachment styles. Safety feels conditional. Connection becomes a negotiation, not a gift.

Agape love is different, not because it has no conditions, but because its conditions are permanent, unchanging, and beyond the reach of performance.

For those within the Christian faith, the primary condition is rooted in the very identity of every person. We are made in God's image, loved by Him, and held dear for redemption's sake. The foundation isn't someone's behavior, beauty, beliefs, or compatibility. It is the unchanging truth of who they are in God's eyes.

As 2 Peter 3:9 (NIV) reminds us, "He is patient with you, not wanting anyone to perish, but everyone to come to repentance." Agape flows from that heart. We long that not one would be lost, not because they've earned love, but because they are intrinsically worthy of it.

Others may find resonance in the moral clarity of the American Founders, who declared: "We hold these truths to be self-evident, that all men are created equal, that they are endowed by their Creator with certain unalienable Rights, that among these are Life, Liberty, and the pursuit of Happiness."

Though political in origin, this statement echoes a shared human conviction. When we recognize that everyone is entitled to life, liberty, and the pursuit of happiness, love takes on an Agape quality—firm, immovable, unshaken.

People possess intrinsic value and deserve dignity and respect, regardless of what they do or who they are. In this light, Agape becomes not only a spiritual calling but a moral imperative.

Understanding the difference between fleeting and permanent foundations of love matters deeply—not just for the health of our relationships, but for the shape of our whole lives.

When love rests on fragile ground, we feel unsafe, reactive, exhausted. We pull away too quickly or cling too tightly. Fear, bargaining, and withdrawal become the rhythms of our connections.

But when love anchors in something unchanging, we no longer scramble to keep it alive. We can set boundaries without fearing abandonment. We can face conflict without panic. We can remain gentle when the waters get rough—all because love is not up for debate.

Psychologically, this kind of love resembles a secure attachment—an inner sense of safety and worthiness that doesn't depend on others' moods or actions. Secure attachment allows vulnerability without fear, boundaries without rejection, and intimacy without losing yourself.

Agape love is steady, generous, rooted in truth.

This section touches the pain we carry. We often believe the foundation of our love is solid—but is it? We mustn't be so blinded by longing that we ignore an honest look at what truly underpins our love—and that of those around us. Getting this right is crucial.

As a reminder, in the last chapter we explored how our need for love and security is as vital as air or food. Does it make sense to rely on counterfeit love? That would be like breathing fake air or eating phony food. And just like the body weakens on imitation nourishment, the soul shrivels on counterfeit love.

Jesus illustrated foundations perfectly when He described the wise and foolish builders (Matthew 7:24–27, NIV). One built his house on sand; the other on rock. When storms came—and they always do—it wasn't the house's beauty that mattered. Foundations matter.

"The rain came down, the streams rose, and the winds blew and beat against that house; yet it did not fall, because it had its foundation on the rock" (Matthew 7:25, NIV).

That's the call of Agape love, not to be blind or naïve, but to be permanently anchored. Agape doesn't depend on how we feel in the moment but on what we believe about human worth, divine intention, and moral responsibility.

The good news? This powerful love can be learned. It begins with perspective.

Even this love has limits. Truth—not fear—guides where we set boundaries. We don't stop loving when it gets hard; we stay rooted in what lasts. "Above all else, guard your heart, for everything you do flows from it" (Proverbs 4:23, NIV).

Reflection Question

What has my love been resting on? Has it been shaped more by fleeting emotions or by deeper, lasting foundations?

Final Thought

The strength of any love reveals itself over time. Collapse comes when the foundation is temporary.

But love grounded in something eternal—whether divine truth or shared humanity—endures even life's fiercest storms. In that love, we don't just survive; we grow, transform, and begin to reflect the steady, faithful heart of Agape itself.

The real test of any love's foundation is how it shows up in the moments that matter. And sometimes, it's a single moment that reshapes everything. Let me share one that changed how I understand Agape love—not as a concept, but as a living reality.

Pumpkin Pie: A Personal Story

Pumpkin pie was my favorite dessert—a comforting treat that felt safe and familiar. I loved how the smooth filling melted on my tongue, how the warmth of cinnamon and nutmeg wrapped around me like an embrace.

But one day, that sense of comfort shattered.

I eagerly asked for a slice, unaware this moment would teach me a painful lesson about neglect and manipulation. The pie had a thick layer of mold—gray-green, fuzzy, unmistakable. I protested again and again. "It has mold on it," but no one listened. No one even looked my way.

I felt utterly alone. My tears threatened to spill, but there was no one close enough to help me hold them back.

Their eyes slid past me as if I were invisible. I was dismissed, scolded, even pressured to eat it. No one acknowledged the truth—until it was too late.

Gulp. I swallowed every last bite.

Then panic set in. An adult screamed in horror, their voice slicing through the indifference. Chaos followed.

And then, someone stood up for me.

My uncle refused to back down. He insisted I be treated well and taken to the hospital immediately. His words were strong and unwavering—a sharp contrast to the neglect I'd known. It became a showdown. Then I heard the whispers:

"What if they take him away?"

"Then he will live with me."

"What if we don't get him back?"

"Then he will stay here as long as he needs."

"I couldn't respond. I had no words."

I wouldn't fully understand the weight of those words until decades later, deep into my healing journey. But at that moment, I knew one thing: someone saw me. Someone was willing to stand firm when I couldn't protect myself.

Agape love is so powerful it pierces half a century later and still brings tears to my eyes. That's the love and security we were meant to know—for all of us.

Trading the Familiar for the Fulfilling

We all begin this journey wanting the same thing: to be genuinely loved. To be seen, known, embraced for who we are. Somewhere along the way, we build strategies to meet that need.

Some of us give endlessly, hoping to earn love through self-sacrifice. Others retreat inward, wearing a confident exterior to be admired rather than rejected. Still others seek attention or control, afraid that letting go means being forgotten.

These patterns look different, but they grow from the same soil: a longing for safety and love.

Eventually, something shifts. The old ways stop satisfying. The praise feels hollow. The silence feels lonelier. The giving feels one-sided. We realize the love we've been trying to earn or control isn't love at all. It's a substitute. Familiar, maybe, but empty.

And if we're honest, we're tired—tired of hustling for love, tired of chasing connection while feeling more disconnected than ever.

That moment in my life was more than an act of kindness—it was a turning point. Someone didn't just react to a crisis; they stepped into it. They responded to me.

That's what makes Agape love different. It doesn't just notice a need; it moves toward it. It doesn't wait for someone to earn care or prove themselves worthy. It simply loves, without condition.

As Scripture says: "Dear children, let us not love with words or speech but with actions and in truth" (1 John 3:18, NIV). That's what I experienced in that moment. That's what love was always meant to be.

Agape love doesn't manipulate or demand. It doesn't change based on performance. It offers something many of us have never truly encountered: consistency, safety, truth.

It's not a fleeting feeling or a reward for good behavior. It's a steady presence that says, "You matter—not because of what you do, but because of who you are."

That kind of love doesn't just heal relationships. It redefines them.

We're all invited to trade what's familiar for what's fulfilling. To stop reaching for love that runs dry and start receiving a love that never does. And when we receive it, we begin to reflect it, not perfectly, but increasingly.

Once you've tasted real love, the counterfeit loses its grip.

Reflection Question

Have you taken detours through counterfeit love only to glimpse, more clearly, the narrow path you were meant to walk?

Today, try seeing just one person through the lens of Agape—whether as someone created in God's image or simply as a human being entitled to life, liberty, and the pursuit of happiness. Let that perspective shape how you respond—with dignity, compassion, and truth.

Final Thought

Agape is not about finding someone who deserves your love. It is about choosing to love because love itself is right and true. It's a decision anchored in who you are, not in what someone else does.

Understanding Agape love helps us see the difference between genuine care and the ways love can be twisted or imitated. In the next chapter, we'll explore how control and manipulation often masquerade as love—and how to recognize those hidden patterns that undermine true connection.

4

Chapter 3: Recognizing the Many Faces of Control

We all begin with the same longing to be safe and deeply loved. But somewhere along the way, many of us learned a painful bargain: to keep one, we might have to sacrifice the other. In that quiet compromise, control slips in subtly at first, yet powerful enough to shape everything that follows.

Control wears many disguises. It can sound like loyalty, look like care, even feel like love. But true love neither demands nor deceives—it honors. It doesn't pressure or perform; it connects. Sometimes control is loud and obvious: raised voices, ultimatums, relentless demands. Other times, it's almost invisible—a soft pull that makes you second-guess your instincts or edit yourself just to keep the peace.

However it shows up, control tells the same story not of strength, but of fear. And fear doesn't always look like fear. Sometimes it looks like devotion, helpfulness, or even love itself.

In this chapter, we'll uncover how control weaves itself into everyday relationships—how it hides, how it convinces us it's necessary, and how it quietly keeps us from the closeness we crave. For a deeper dive, Appendix A outlines key traits, and Appendix B explores common types.

Why People Manipulate: It's Not What You Think

Control rarely begins with cruelty. More often, it starts with fear—fear of rejection, fear of being left behind, fear of being truly seen. It can look like devotion, helpfulness, or constant attentiveness. But beneath it all is an ache for security, desperately trying to keep the connection from slipping away.

In psychology, this is called coercive control—the attempt to shape another person's emotions, choices, or behavior to feel safe. It might use flattery, guilt, silence, charm, or misdirection. The tactics vary, but the goal is the same: to avoid the rawness of vulnerability by reaching for control.

Scripture names this clearly: "For where you have envy and selfish ambition, there you find disorder and every evil practice" (James 3:16, NIV). Even when it masquerades as love, manipulation grows from self-interest and fear.

But fear doesn't have to have the last word. Naming what's beneath the behavior begins to change everything. Control may feel like protection, but it pushes away the very closeness we crave. And for the one on the receiving end, it can feel disorienting—like trying to find your way through a maze blindfolded while struggling not to let anyone down.

The Distorted Pursuit of Love and Safety

At its root, manipulation grows out of a fear-based misunderstanding: If I don't fight for love, I'll lose it. If I don't manage everything, I won't be safe. These beliefs often go unnamed, yet they shape entire relational patterns. Families, cultures, even churches sometimes confuse control with care. It's a conclusion many of us reached early, often without realizing it.

But fear cannot produce love.

This belief shapes our behaviors: earning approval, managing impressions, and working tirelessly to stay in someone's good graces. One common pattern is intermittent reinforcement—a push-pull cycle of kindness and withdrawal that breeds confusion and anxiety. We hope. We doubt. We overfunction, trying to close the gap.

Most of the time, this story begins in childhood. Maybe love felt conditional. Perhaps approval had to be earned. The connection might have been inconsistent. So we learned to try harder, to manage emotions—ours and others—in the hope that no one would leave.

But what once helped us survive eventually isolates us. What once looked like strength may actually be a shield. And the cycle of control eventually blocks the very love it was trying to protect.

Uncontrolled Love: A Fictional Story

Mark grew up in a home where affection was tied to behavior. Praise came with performance. Criticism came quickly when he fell short. As an adult, he became what many would call dependable—always anticipating needs, avoiding conflict, staying one step ahead.

People praised his consistency. But Mark was anxious. When someone pulled away or needed space, he tightened his hold—more messages, more gestures, more control. He wasn't trying to manipulate. He simply didn't know another way to feel secure.

Then he met Emma. She didn't ask for more effort. She asked for honesty. One evening, she said gently, "Mark, love isn't a reward system. You don't have to hold people in place to keep them. Love isn't afraid of freedom."

That conversation shifted something. Over time, Mark began to see his patterns not as care, but as fear dressed up as devotion. He started practicing letting go—not all at once, but in small, deliberate ways. And in that letting go, he felt something unfamiliar: real connection.

Mark's story reminds us that love rooted in fear isn't love. It's a contract. And contracts can't create the freedom love needs to thrive.

What Can You Try Instead?

If any part of that story feels familiar—or simply human—you're not alone. Control is one of the oldest survival strategies. But so is healing.

If you're curious about another way, here are a few small steps:

- **Notice, don't judge.** When you feel the urge to fix or manage someone else's reaction, pause and ask: "What am I trying to protect right now?"
- **Try a small release.** Let a text go unanswered a little longer. Let someone else carry the emotional weight of a decision. Let go of the need to explain every no.
- **Replace control with curiosity**. Instead of rehearsing how to prevent disappointment, ask: "What are you feeling right now? What would bring more peace to this moment?"

These shifts don't have to be big to be real. Even one moment of letting go makes space for love to show up in a new way.

Love Was Never Meant to Be This Way

"There is no fear in love. But perfect love drives out fear,
because fear has to do with punishment."
1 John 4:18, NIV

When fear drives love, it becomes something else—anxious, conditional, unsafe.

But the kind of love that heals doesn't grip. It doesn't perform. It doesn't punish. It rests. It trusts. It invites.

Scripture doesn't just call out manipulation as wrong; it reveals what it does to the human heart: "The acts of the flesh are obvious: sexual immorality, impurity and debauchery; idolatry and witchcraft; hatred, discord, jealousy, fits of rage, selfish ambition, dissensions, factions and envy; I warn you, as I did before, that those who live like this will not inherit the kingdom of God" (Galatians 5:19–21, NIV).

Regardless of faith, these patterns fracture relationships. They turn connection into transactions. And they don't just harm others—they rob us internally of peace, intimacy, and joy. They promise protection but leave us isolated.

Reflection Question

Where in your relationships do you feel the urge to hold on tightly? What techniques are you using to hold on?

Final Thought

Control is a natural instinct when love feels uncertain. But the love you were made for isn't earned through effort or preserved through pressure. It doesn't need a grip to survive. It simply needs space to breathe.

The freedom you're longing for doesn't come after you hold it all together. It comes the moment you're willing to let go.

But what if control doesn't even wear the mask we expect? What if it hides behind care, affection, or even love itself? In the next section, we'll uncover how manipulation often disguises itself as love—transactions that feel like connection but quietly steal it away.

Manipulation as a Transaction that Mimics Love

Building on our earlier exploration of control, let's take a closer look at how manipulation often cloaks itself as love. These behaviors can feel comforting—especially for those who've learned that affection must be earned. But they aren't love. They're transactions.

This kind of love is conditional. It offers approval only when you conform—and withdraws it when you don't. Reward and punishment. Counterfeit affection. Over time, this erodes confidence, breeds confusion, and traps you in a relentless cycle of performance.

Scripture warns us about this kind of deceit: "Wounds from a friend can be trusted, but an enemy multiplies kisses" (Proverbs 27:6, NIV). Not every kiss signals care. Not every compliment is kindness. Manipulation often wraps control in affectionate packaging—just believable enough to feel like love, just convincing enough to keep you hooked.

Tactics That Feel Like Love (But Aren't)

Here are a couple of specific behaviors that masquerade as connection but serve as control.

"Love bombing", often found in the early stages of a relationship, overwhelms you with attention, gifts, and intense words of affirmation. It feels thrilling—almost miraculous. But the aim isn't closeness. It's control.

Once the manipulator feels secure, the warmth fades. Affection turns to withdrawal. Compliments turn to criticism. Then the affection may return. You're left wondering, "What happened?"

"Trauma bonding" is a term psychologists use for a cycle—a back-and-forth of emotional highs and lows that creates a powerful psychological hook. These brief moments of warmth function like breadcrumbs, keeping you chasing what once felt real.

Jesus warned us to look beyond appearances: "Watch out for false prophets. They come to you in sheep's clothing, but inwardly they are ferocious wolves" (Matthew 7:15, NIV). Intense early affection isn't proof of genuine love—it can be a red flag.

"Mirroring" is a technique where the manipulator reflects your values, interests, and personality as if they were their own. The mirror creates the illusion of deep compatibility:

E: "I love hiking in the mountains."

N: "No way, me too! Nature clears my mind."

E: "I've always dreamed of working with kids."

N: "Same! I've wanted that since I was little."

It feels like being truly seen. But often, it's a performance designed to accelerate attachment. Once trust is secured, the mirroring fades—and true motives emerge.

Real love celebrates differences and grows slowly. Manipulative mirroring bypasses that natural process. It's less about knowing you and more about shaping you into a predictable source of supply.

To spot mirroring in real time, try this: when someone repeats your thoughts or feelings too quickly or perfectly, pause and ask yourself, "Is this genuine interest, or a rehearsed reflection?"

Love That Was Never Real: A Fictional Story

Emma had never felt so wanted. Jason was charming, attentive, and intuitive. He texted her good morning and good night. He showed up with her favorite coffee. He said the words she'd always longed to hear.

But after a few months, the sparkle dimmed. When she voiced concerns, Jason withdrew. When she asked for more time together, he responded with cold logic: "I've been busy. You're too emotional."

Then, just as she was ready to walk away, he reappeared with sweetness again: "I miss you, babe. You're everything to me."

Emma felt like she was caught in a relentless tide—pulled up by warmth, then dragged down by distance. When she finally stepped back, she realized what she thought was love had been control all along.

Why This Works (And Why It's So Hard to Leave)

Manipulation that mimics love often works because it meets a deep longing for safety and connection. When someone showers us with affection or approval, it ignites hope—especially if we're accustomed to counterfeit care.

But that same longing can keep us trapped. We whisper, "Maybe it will go back to the beginning," or "If I try harder, the kindness will return."

The relationship becomes like a slot machine—occasional rewards keep us pulling the lever, even as we lose ourselves.

This isn't a sign of weakness. It means your longing for love is powerful. And that longing isn't the problem. The problem is when it's exploited.

This longing for love, the same deep desire at the heart of all healthy connection, is the very thing manipulation preys upon—turning your hope into chains.

From the manipulator's side, many don't wake up planning to control anyone. They're often wounded themselves, operating from a belief that they must earn closeness, that power keeps them safe, or that honesty would make them unlovable.

Some may meet criteria for disorders like narcissistic personality disorder. Others simply get stuck in unquestioned patterns.

Psychology may say some of these individuals are unlikely to change. But faith opens a door psychology alone cannot. Healing is possible. Repentance is available. But change requires willingness—and not everyone will choose it.

As we'll explore in future chapters, your freedom does not depend on their transformation. You have the authority to walk away from false love, even if they never admit what they've done.

Recognizing manipulation that mimics love is painful. It can feel like betrayal. You may grieve not just the relationship, but the version of love you thought you had. That grief is sacred. It means your heart still longs for the real thing.

The goal isn't to become jaded. It's to become wise. Jesus promises: "Then you will know the truth, and the truth will set you free" (John 8:32, NIV).

Action Plan

To grow in discernment, start by identifying patterns, not just moments. Look for the cycles that repeat. Explore the traits listed in Appendix A to sharpen your awareness.

If these patterns describe someone in your life, try this:

- When they push for control or affection on their terms, gently remind yourself you're not responsible for fixing them.
- Practice saying no or stepping back with kindness and firmness.
- Reach out to trusted friends, counselors, or mentors who can help you stay grounded.

If these patterns describe you, remember: you're not alone, or defined by them. These traits are signals from your wounded heart, inviting you toward healing and growth. Be gentle with yourself. Change is a journey, not a sudden fix.

As we'll explore later in this book, you can rewrite your story.

Reflection Question

Who in your life shows affection that feels conditional or controlling? What specific patterns keep repeating?

Final Thought

Manipulation often hides behind sweet words and dramatic gestures. But love that must be earned or performed isn't love. It's survival.

In the next section, we'll take a closer look at the forms of control manipulators often use, covert and overt. Recognizing these patterns helps you protect your peace and choose love that's real.

Covert and Overt Control: Recognizing the Signs

Manipulation wears many faces—sometimes loud and demanding, other times soft and seemingly sweet. But whether whispered or shouted, it twists relationships in painful ways. To name it clearly, we first need to understand its two main faces: covert and overt.

Both forms use different tactics, yet they share the same motive—avoiding vulnerability while maintaining control. When you recognize these patterns, you move from confusion to clarity. That clarity is the first step toward freedom.

At its root, manipulation is fear dressed up as connection—a heart trying to stay safe by managing others instead of reaching for love.

Covert Manipulation: The Quiet Mask

Covert manipulation hides behind kindness, politeness, or even spiritual language. It avoids open confrontation, relying on subtle tactics like guilt, flattery, or passive aggression to shape outcomes.

Think of the sigh that says, "You disappointed me, without a single word." Or concern wrapped in control: "I'm just worried. People might get the wrong idea."

Some even twist Scripture or prayer into pressure, using spiritual language to silence, shame, or steer others. They may appear devout or noble, but beneath the surface is a drive to dominate. This is the heart of spiritual narcissism—using religion to elevate self, evade accountability, or enforce conformity.

Jesus confronted this directly: "Everything they do is done for people to see. They love the place of honor at banquets" (Matthew 23:5–6, NIV). People like this confuse holiness with hierarchy and conviction with control.

If you've been wounded by this kind of manipulation—especially inside a faith community, your skepticism makes sense. You may not have walked away from God, only from those who misrepresented Him. If that's you, consider this a gentle re-invitation: Jesus didn't control others. He healed. He listened. He invited. He never used fear to keep followers or twisted truth to gain power.

For more on spiritual narcissism—how to spot it, name it, and heal—see Appendix B.

Narcissism in the Church

Since we're already on this topic, let's go a little deeper. While all are invited and welcome in church, should unrepentant narcissists be in a position of influence—which may include leadership—in a church? Here the key word is "unrepentant"—one not seriously seeking improvement in moving beyond narcissistic traits.

Scripture addresses this concern: "As for a person who stirs up division, after warning him once and then twice, have nothing more to do with him" (Titus 3:10, NIV).

It even names this as a sign of the times: "In the last days there will come times of difficulty. For people will be lovers of themselves, lovers of money, proud, arrogant, abusive, disobedient to their parents, ungrateful, unholy, without love, having a form of godliness but denying its power. Avoid such people" (2 Timothy 3:1–5, NIV).

And it reminds leaders how they're meant to serve: "Not domineering over those in your charge, but being examples to the flock" (1 Peter 5:3, NIV).

Those not seeking to discover or grow their faith really do not belong in a church and especially not in positions of influence or leadership. Boundaries aren't just wise—they're biblical. The church is meant to be a refuge for those genuinely seeking God, not a stage for those who twist His name for personal gain.

Overt Manipulation: The Loud Command

Overt manipulation is easier to spot: bold, pressuring, and often laced with anger. These manipulators use volume, fear, or ultimatums to force compliance:

- "You'd better not walk away from me."
- "If you loved me, you'd do this right now."
- "Don't make me regret trusting you."

Proverbs gives a clear warning: "Do not make friends with a hot-tempered person or you may learn their ways and get yourself ensnared" (Proverbs 22:24–25, NIV).

Overt manipulators may use logic, shame, or even spiritual guilt, but what's always missing is freedom. Their desire for control outweighs your right to think, feel, or choose differently. Underneath, these behaviors often spring from entitlement: I know best or You owe me. Even when they appear confident, overt manipulators are often driven by deep insecurity and fear of rejection.

Manipulation Often Shifts Forms

One of the most confusing parts of manipulation is how quickly it changes shape. Someone who seemed tender may suddenly turn cold, angry, or aggressive when they don't get their way. That shift leaves you doubting yourself: Did I imagine the kindness? Was it my fault they exploded?

Psychologists call this an extinction burst—a surge in manipulative behavior when control is threatened. Ironically, this often means your boundary is working.

From Soft Control to Sharp Pressure: A Fictional Story

Melissa had always been the peacemaker. For her, silence felt safer than honesty. When she felt hurt, she didn't speak up. She dropped subtle hints, hoping her husband, Daniel, would read between the lines. When he didn't, she retreated into silence.

But when Daniel stopped reacting, Melissa escalated.

"You never listen. Maybe I should just stop trying."

One night, her sorrow turned into a storm. She wept, raised her voice, and blurted something she didn't mean:

"You make me feel worthless!"

Daniel was stunned—not just by her pain, but by the sudden whiplash. He felt compassion for her sadness, but also a dawning realization: the tenderness he once saw as vulnerability had become a tool to shape his reactions, manage his choices, and guard her fears.

In that moment, Daniel saw he'd been responding not to honest communication but to emotional cues and unspoken rules. The kindness he once cherished had strings attached.

They both had work to do. But the first step was naming the behavior.

Quick Red Flags

You may be dealing with covert or overt manipulation if you notice:

- **Feeling guilt or confusion** after basic conversations;
- **Second-guessing** yourself to keep the peace;
- **Compliance praise** praise received only when you comply;
- **Boundaries** tested or ignored;
- **Fearing** to express disagreement;
- **Pressure** For example experiencing Scripture or spiritual ideas used as pressure;
- **Walking on eggshells** around someone prone to outbursts; or
- **Similar** - re-read these and notice how they shape a funnel that you need to follow, but is not of your choice.

These aren't accusations. They're invitations to pay attention. You are being shaped into someone that perhaps you were not meant to be.

What to Do When You See the Pattern

Recognizing manipulation isn't about blame. It's about reclaiming freedom.

Try these practical steps:

- **Pause before reacting.** Don't rush to explain or appease.
- **Name what's happening.** This feels like pressure, not a request.
- **Set a boundary.** You don't need permission to protect your peace.

- **Refuse to play.** Step out of guilt traps or power games.
- **Ask for clarity.** Invite God to show you what's true—not just what's familiar.

More on these practical steps to come. Remember Jesus' words: "Let your Yes be Yes, and your No, No; anything beyond this comes from the evil one" (Matthew 5:37, NIV).

Truth doesn't twist. Love doesn't push.

Reflection Question

Have you noticed shifting patterns of manipulation in someone close to you—or in yourself? How might you respond? What do you think about the suggestions in Appendix B?

Final Thought

Whether the mask is velvet or iron, manipulation still controls. But love without fear is possible. You don't have to keep dancing the same painful steps. A new rhythm is calling—led not by control, but by truth, wisdom, and peace.

Next, we'll look more closely at specific traits and tactics so you can spot manipulators with greater ease.

Spotting Manipulation: Traits, Types, and Tactics

Now that we've named the forms manipulation can take—covert and overt—it's time to look closer. Some tactics are loud and obvious. Others are quiet, subtle, and disguised as concern or care. But all manipulation follows a pattern: it steers outcomes while avoiding vulnerability.

We're not blaming as we begin to recognize these patterns in ourselves or others. We're seeking clarity—the kind that leads to peace, courage, and change.

What Makes Manipulation So Dangerous?

More than confusion, manipulation disorients. It twists the fabric of connection. It replaces freedom with control, honesty with illusion. And it often hides behind politeness, spirituality, or good intentions.

At its core, manipulation is a web of coercive tactics—dishonest, indirect, or pressuring—meant to steer someone's feelings, thoughts, or choices. It might shout or whisper. It might use guilt, silence, or shame. But the goal remains the same—control without exposure.

Scripture speaks directly to this: "Then we will no longer be infants, tossed back and forth by the waves. Instead, speaking the truth in love, we will grow to become in every respect the mature body of him who is the head, that is, Christ" (Ephesians 4:14–15, NIV). Manipulation keeps us adrift—but truth in love anchors us to solid ground.

So, how does this show up in real life? For a deeper look at specific manipulative traits—like gaslighting, guilt-tripping, shaming, and passive-aggressiveness—Appendices A and B offer clear descriptions, real-life examples, and gracious scripts to help you name what's happening without losing your grounding in love.

Here, let's examine one of manipulation's most complex tactics and what it takes to recognize and resist it.

Flying Monkeys and Triangulation

Triangulation is a tactic where someone brings in a third party—often called a flying monkey (think Wizard of Oz)—to influence a situation without facing it directly.

It may look like venting or asking for support. But underneath, it's about steering the narrative or shifting pressure.

Have you ever found yourself caught between two people's unspoken conflict? Or been drawn into someone's pain before they addressed it with the person involved? These moments can seem innocent—but they're often emotional smokescreens for indirect control.

This kind of influence damages more than just the relationship at the center. It creates confusion, spreads doubt, and divides trust. Proverbs 6:16–19 (NIV) gives a strong warning: "There are six things the Lord hates, seven that are detestable to him, and a person who stirs up conflict in the community." That last line is a picture of triangulation—conflict stirred by those unwilling to confront it honestly and directly.

Larry, Ted, and a Town Torn: A Fictional Story

Larry and Ted had been friends in a small town where everyone knew each other's business. When Ted started setting boundaries—seeking space and calm—Larry grew resentful but didn't confront him directly.

Instead, Larry began tracking Ted's movements around town, visiting places Ted usually went. He spun a story mixed with truth and falsehood, portraying himself as the victim and Ted as cold and untrustworthy.

Small-town gossip spread quickly. Some people pulled away from Ted, and others avoided his company. Most ignored the charade. Ted did not bother sharing the truth with those in town who preferred gossip over grace. For those folks, there was no room for truth when Larry had juicy smears to share.

The rumors damaged relationships, businesses lost customers, and tensions rose. Trust and the community were left broken. Larry never did succeed in crossing Ted's boundary.

Evil often creeps in through unchecked stories—leaving a trail of destruction in its wake. But God sees what is hidden and weighs every heart. "The Lord detests lying lips, but he delights in people who are trustworthy" (Proverbs 12:22, NIV).

Can you see how a church might allow abominations inside its doors? Imagine the tarnishing and spiritually disruptive effect of letting Larry tell his tales unchecked within a church. How would Ted respond to such a community? Might he see the entire church as a den of flying monkeys? And how would God respond? "There are six things the Lord hates, seven that are detestable to him, and a person who stirs up conflict in the community" (Proverbs 6:16–19, NIV).

Yet, even in the face of slander and division, God offers a better way. Truth can still be spoken. Hearts can still turn. Communities can still choose repentance over ruin. And those who have been harmed can find refuge in Him, the One who defends the innocent and restores what was broken.

Why It Works

As the story shows, triangulation feels safer than direct confrontation. It avoids exposure and keeps the initiator in control. But the cost is high: fractured trust, strained relationships, and disconnection masked as concern.

What's tricky is that many who use triangulation don't recognize it. They may be trying to process pain or protect a fragile sense of self. But even with good intentions, the result is the same—confusion, division, and quiet pressure.

Scripture and psychology both name this pattern. Galatians 5:19–21 (NIV) warns that selfish ambition and discord destroy sacred connection. And psychology names it coercive control—indirect influence that limits another person's freedom.

In both cases, the root is the same—fear.

How to Respond to Manipulation

When manipulation surfaces, our first instinct is often to react, explain, defend, or fight back. But healing begins with restraint. Clarity doesn't rush. It stands still and sees.

Whether you approach this from a faith lens, a psychological one, or both, here are practical ways to break the cycle:

- **Pause and disengage.** Let the manipulative behavior unfold without jumping in. Your silence can hold power. "The peace of God, which transcends all understanding, will guard your hearts and your minds in Christ Jesus" (Philippians 4:7, NIV).
- **Name the tactic gently.** Use calm, non-accusatory language: "It feels like you're asking me to pass this message along, or that sounds like pressure." Colossians 3:9–10 shares: "Do not lie to each other but put on the new self, renewed in knowledge in the image of its Creator." (NIV).
- **Delay decisions.** Manipulators often create false urgency. You can create space by saying, "I need to think about it." Boundaries don't need permission.
- **Invite clarity.** Ask, "What exactly are you asking?" or "Will you talk to them directly?" Encourage open dialogue.
- **Step out of the triangle.** Refuse to carry messages or choose sides. Redirect with grace: "That's something you should share with them directly."
- **Seek community.** Trusted allies can help reflect the truth when your view gets clouded.
- **Pray for wisdom.** Psalm 139:23 (NIV) offers this honest prayer: "Search me, God, and know my heart; test me and know my anxious thoughts."

There isn't always is there a solution, and sometimes you need to just leave the situation.

Reflection

Sometimes we recognize manipulation in others. Other times, we see it in ourselves. That doesn't make us bad—it makes us human. Most of us were shaped by environments where control felt safer than truth and silence felt easier than vulnerability.

Have you noticed moments when you've avoided conflict by involving someone else—what feelings were behind that choice? These questions are invitations to awareness.

This week, pay careful attention. Manipulation can be inherited, practiced, or reflexive. But when we see it clearly, we can choose differently. And that choice opens the door to healing—for us and those around us.

Final Thought

Manipulation thrives in hidden agendas, but love welcomes light. It invites truth, nurtures freedom, and opens space for transformation.

Isaiah 41:10 (NIV) reminds us: "So do not fear, for I am with you; do not be dismayed, for I am your God. I will strengthen you and help you." That strength isn't for domination—it's for wholeness.

You don't have to keep dancing the exhausting steps of discomfort and control. A new rhythm is calling—one led by wisdom, grounded in truth, and rooted in love.

As we close this chapter, remember: control wears many faces, and manipulation often hides behind care or conflict. Recognizing these patterns is the first step toward freedom and authentic connection.

Next, we'll explore the beautiful burden of deep sensitivity—the challenges and gifts of those who feel deeply—and why understanding this dynamic is key to breaking free from the toxic dance.

5

Chapter 4: The Beautiful Burden of Deep Sensitivity

You walk into a room, and before anyone speaks, you feel it. The air hums with unspoken tension—anger, sadness, anxiety. Without realizing it, those emotions slip beneath your skin.

That's empathy.

Some move through life largely untouched by the moods of others. But if you're like me, you read the room instinctively. You sense shifts others miss. Sometimes it's hard to tell where their feelings end and yours begin. It's not just sensitivity—it's absorption.

Empathy is a profound strength. It connects. It comforts. It heals. Yet when misunderstood or unguarded, it can drain, confuse, and blur boundaries. This chapter explores that paradox—the beauty and burden of deep sensitivity—and how it transforms when paired with wisdom.

Why Deep Feelers Both Struggle and Shine

Here's the good news: empathy isn't merely a trait; it's a skill. While it comes naturally to some, it can also be cultivated and stewarded. You're not doomed to live at the mercy of every emotion—yours or anyone else's.

At the heart of human connection, people tend to engage in one of two ways: with self-focus or other-focus. Empaths tilt toward others. We don't just understand emotions—we carry them. We feel the tension before anyone speaks. We comfort without needing words. And sometimes, long after the conversation ends, we still carry its weight.

That constant pull to help can overwhelm you, especially if you don't know how to release what was never yours.

Psychologists often call this heightened sensitivity being a Highly Sensitive Person (HSP). Research suggests it may be linked to more active mirror neurons—brain cells that help us attune emotionally to others. These neurons allow for deep connection but can also lead to emotional overload. Over time, constant exposure to stress or negativity blurs the line between what belongs to you and what doesn't.

No wonder many empaths become people-pleasers. They twist themselves into knots to meet expectations, terrified that boundaries will cost them love. What begins as compassion morphs into survival.

But not all empaths seek to be liked. Some remain silent for a different reason—they're not seeking approval but peace. Peacemakers often surrender their own voice to avoid conflict. Their motives may be noble, but when harmony becomes more important than integrity, even good intentions become self-abandonment.

Scripture calls us to a healthier empathy: "Rejoice with those who rejoice; mourn with those who mourn" (Romans 12:15, NIV). We're invited to meet people where they are—but not to become their sorrow.

I learned this the hard way. For years, I thought love meant giving until I had nothing left. But love isn't depletion. Love is presence. It stays near without disappearing into someone else's pain.

That's why Galatians 6:5 (NIV) is essential: "For each one should carry their own load." We're called to support one another, yes—but not to carry what was never ours. Taking responsibility for someone else's life isn't compassion. It's exhaustion.

"The prudent see danger and take refuge, but the simple keep going and pay the penalty" (Proverbs 22:3, NIV). Discernment is love in action. When your body senses unease, don't dismiss it. That internal signal may be protection.

The Intersection with Agape Love

Empaths often strive to embody Agape—selfless love. But when compassion lacks boundaries, even Agape can become distorted. What starts as sacrificial can quietly become self-destructive.

True Agape doesn't demand you abandon yourself. It gives with wisdom, not guilt. It embraces others while still honoring the self. It flows from peace, not anxiety.

Love becomes heavy when offered out of fear or the need to prove you're enough. But when sensitivity is paired with discernment, love becomes clear again—still rich in compassion, but no longer driven by performance.

One of the most overlooked forms of discernment is noticing not just what is said, but how it's said. Deep feelers pick up on the emotional music beneath the words—the tone, cadence, and posture. We sense the difference between humility and pride, love and control, empathy and manipulation.

Over time, this sensitivity sharpens into intuition. It becomes almost spiritual. You begin to see how narcissism rushes, dominates, persuades. Pride feels heavy and loud. Control presses forward. But genuine empathy makes space. Humility moves slowly. Love listens. It doesn't force—it invites.

As you learn to trust what you sense, discomfort turns into clarity. And clarity becomes courage. That's the beginning of wisdom.

Practicing Wisdom as an Empath

When you sense heaviness, pause. Don't rush to fix or absorb it. Simply notice.

Then ask yourself gently: "Is this mine?"

Ask again, with honesty: "Is this mine to carry—or am I stepping into a space I was never invited to cross?"

Let your body guide you. Notice if you feel a tightening in your chest, a clouding of your thoughts, or a rush of urgency. Pressure, confusion, and false urgency are often spiritual red flags.

When you feel that pull, anchor yourself in truth: "Each should carry their own load" (Galatians 6:5, NIV).

And when the guilt tries to creep in, remind yourself—boundaries are not selfish. They're an expression of love.

The Warning Signal: A Fictional Story

Alyssa could always sense a shift before it surfaced. It wasn't magic—it was a hard-earned awareness that had protected her more times than she could count.

At a friend's gathering, she met Daniel. He was charming, attentive on the surface, perfect. But something in her chest tightened. His eyes felt hollow. His kindness felt rehearsed.

As the evening wore on, Alyssa noticed how he redirected every conversation. He offered shallow concern, then reclaimed the spotlight. He gently tested boundaries, watching her reactions.

She knew this feeling. She'd ignored it before. And she had paid dearly.

Not this time.

When Daniel turned his charm toward her, Alyssa smiled but didn't yield. She trusted what she sensed. She walked away whole.

Her sensitivity was no longer a liability. It was her strength. Her protection.

The Weight of Expectation: A Personal Story

Law school became a turning point for me, but the pressure to over-deliver lingered. I gave too much, met unrealistic demands, and often acted from fear.

Then I asked myself: If I stopped over-delivering, would anyone still care?

The answer hurt. Some people disappeared. Others grew frustrated. But the ones who truly loved me stayed.

That's when I learned: love has nothing to do with performance. People either choose to love you or they don't. Their choice speaks more about them than you.

And you have a choice too—who to let in, and on what terms.

That's when I found it: love that isn't earned is the only love worth keeping. Agape love.

Empathy without boundaries isn't compassion. It's self-neglect. Learning to distinguish genuine care from fear allowed me to choose relationships that nourished me instead of draining me.

Reflection Question

Have you ever confused compassion with self-sacrifice in a way that left you feeling empty? What would you change if you could relive that moment?

Final Thought

Navigating life as an empath means pairing sensitivity with strength. Don't shut down your empathy to stay safe. Grow confident in it.

Stay open, but stay rooted. Cultivate compassion that listens without losing your voice and give without losing yourself.

You don't have to carry everything to care deeply. Sensitivity, when stewarded with wisdom, becomes more than a gift—it becomes a ministry. It heals others, and by God's grace, it heals you too.

How Sensitivity Shows Up and Why It Matters

Sensitivity shows up differently in everyone. Often, it expresses itself through empathy—the ability to feel what others feel and respond with care. But not all empathy looks the same. Some express it outwardly, with visible compassion and comforting words. Others carry it subtly, often unnoticed, but no less powerful. This softer form is called covert empathy.

Covert Empathy: Gentle Strength

Covert empathy doesn't seek recognition. It runs deep, often moving without outward display. Those who lead with covert empathy support others through presence, timing, and small, deliberate gestures of care that often go unseen.

Often aligned with peacemakers, covert empaths avoid the spotlight. They cultivate harmony behind the scenes. Their compassion emerges through thoughtful gestures, private encouragement, or simply sitting beside someone in stillness. These expressions are powerful in their humility.

Covert empathy reflects the spirit Jesus praised when He said, "Blessed are the meek, for they will inherit the earth" (Matthew 5:5, NIV). Meekness isn't weakness. It's strength under control—humility in motion. Love without applause.

Yet in our culture—and sometimes in the church—we tend to overlook or undervalue this love. We praise big expressions and loud affirmations but forget that true power often moves quietly. Covert empaths sense what others miss—and choose to respond anyway.

Covert empathy also leans on intuition. A covert empath often feels pain, fear, or joy—even when no words are spoken. They move toward those who are hurting, not to fix, but to offer comfort in ways that feel natural and unobtrusive.

A Moment That Mattered: A Personal Story

I remember watching a live YouTube show where a guest speaker received harsh comments. I noticed a shift—shoulders drawing inward, a pause before responding. Most would have missed it, but I felt it immediately.

So I typed a quick comment into the chat for the guest: "While a few may disagree, the rest of us love you and want to hear more."

The speaker glanced at the message, and her posture softened. A small smile returned. She spoke with more ease. Later, she didn't remember the exchange, but I did. And I saw how it helped.

That's covert empathy—unseen, yet unmistakably authentic. It doesn't demand attention or chase applause. It simply shows up when it matters most.

You don't have to be loud to make a difference. Sometimes, the softest voices carry the most love.

Overt Empathy: Open and Public

In contrast, overt empathy is visible. Expressive. Public. Overt empaths speak their care out loud. They act quickly, comfort openly, and advocate directly. Their empathy is evident, active, and often becomes a rallying point.

For overt empaths, the impulse comes from within—a desire to connect through action. They don't just feel empathy; they display it. They draw people together by offering support in unmistakable, heartfelt ways.

An example of overt empathy is Jesus washing the disciples' feet. In John 13:1–17 (NIV), Jesus offers a striking example of overt empathy. He washes His disciples' feet. This was an act few expected, but none forgot. He didn't do it in private. He made it visible. He didn't just speak of love. He showed it.

That moment wasn't obligation. It was presence. His empathy became action. And His action became an eternal example of love moving beyond words.

The Connection Between Covert and Overt Empathy

Covert and overt empathy may seem like opposites, but they often live within the same person. One may lead with covert empathy in reflective settings, then shift to overt empathy when the moment calls for it. Both arise from genuine care; neither is rooted in arrogance.

In a group, one may quietly slip a note of encouragement, while another organizes a gathering to lift someone's spirits. Both were born from empathy. One private and still. The other public and active. Jesus modeled both.

Types of Empaths

Different empaths may favor one expression. Psychology identifies common types to include:

- **Emotional Empaths:** Deeply tuned to feelings. May offer covert comfort or overt support.
- **Intuitive Empaths:** Sense needs before they're spoken. Act on what others haven't voiced.
- **Nature Empaths:** Connected to creation—animals, plants. Empathy may show as stewardship or advocacy. Does a walk in the woods soothe you?
- **Physical Empaths:** Feel others' physical pain. Often drawn to hands-on comfort or healing.
- **Mental Empaths:** Sense someone's thoughts before they speak. They don't interrupt—they understand. They offer strategy, insight, or presence without needing to explain it.

To me, these feel like artificial boundaries, although there may be areas where we more easily connect. Jesus seemed to carry all forms. Notice how often He withdrew to natural places to pray and reconnect. Perhaps that tells us something about how sensitivity is restored.

Practical Insight: Why Knowing Your Empath Type Matters

Understanding your empath type(s) shifts how you connect and interpret others. For example, if you're more of a physical empath married to a spouse that is more of a mental empath, you may long for touch while they prefer quiet processing.

One couple I know struggled with this. She felt abandoned when he withdrew; he felt overwhelmed when she reached out. Recognizing their different empath types shifted everything. They asked new questions, listened with grace, and stretched toward each other.

Misunderstandings often come not from lack of love but different languages of care. Awareness softens frustration. It invites compassion and builds bridges.

Instead of assuming withdrawal means rejection or closeness means pressure, we learn wiring—and extend patience.

Sometimes, this understanding invites us to pause and ask: How can I meet others in their unique way? How can I adjust my response to honor their needs without sacrificing my own?

A Reflection on Empathy and the Divine

Empathy is more than human sensitivity—it reflects the heart of God, who is relational by nature. In His triune existence, God models perfect empathy—listening, responding, and moving with love toward His Creation.

When we practice empathy well, we participate in that divine dance, becoming co-workers in healing and restoration. Each act of compassionate presence echoes an invitation: Come, walk with me in love that transforms.

Reflection Question

Take a moment now. Close your eyes and breathe deeply. Reflect on a recent interaction where you felt deeply moved by someone's emotions. Did you respond privately or openly? What type of empath were you in that instance? Now imagine honoring that style—trusting your natural way of caring as a gift, not a burden. How might this awareness change your next interaction? Keep this awareness with you today, and notice how your empathy shapes connection and healing.

How do you express empathy—covertly, overtly, or a mix? What does that reveal about how you naturally connect?

Final Thought

Empathy is multifaceted. Whispered or spoken aloud, it flows from care—the desire to ease suffering, the choice to walk alongside. There's no single right way to love well. What matters is showing up—genuinely, intentionally, humbly.

When empathy is grounded in truth and guided by discernment, it becomes more than feeling. It becomes transformation—for you and for those you love.

Empathy vs. Enabling: The Challenge of Boundaries

Empathy connects us deeply to others. It lets us share burdens and show up in people's darkest moments. But when that care turns into quiet self-erasure, something essential is lost. The line between caring and overextending is often imperceptible—especially for those who feel others' pain as intensely as their own. For empaths, that line is not just blurred; it's nearly invisible.

This sensitivity, while a gift, can also become a trap. Empathy mutates into enabling when helping others becomes a way to preserve connection or avoid conflict. The consequences start subtly: emotional fatigue, vague resentment, or an unshakeable sense of being unseen. Over time, the toll grows heavier. What began as compassion slowly erodes the self.

Why Empaths Struggle to Walk Away

Empaths are wired to feel. They don't merely observe suffering—they absorb it. This deep emotional resonance fuels a fierce desire to heal what's broken, to stand beside someone no one else would, to be the one who stays.

That devotion is noble. But it also makes empaths especially vulnerable to unhealthy dynamics.

When an empath's sense of worth hinges on their ability to soothe others, boundaries begin to vanish. The fear of being seen as cold becomes a heavy burden. For many, walking away from a toxic relationship doesn't feel like self-preservation—it feels like failure. They worry that if they leave, no one else will stay. That belief, born from compassion, becomes a prison.

Jesus' words in Mark 12:31, "Love your neighbor as yourself," offer crucial insight. This command is often quoted but not always fully grasped. When "as yourself" is read as equal measure, love drifts into transactional patterns—but Agape love, the love Jesus models, simultaneously cares for self and other together, without barter or self-erasure. True love involves caring for others and for ourselves. Without both, love becomes unbalanced. When empaths prioritize someone else's comfort over their own well-being, they upset this delicate balance. What appears as love on the surface can become emotional servitude—honoring neither God nor health.

This tension between love and loss is more than spiritual—it's psychological, too. Studies show highly empathetic individuals are particularly prone to people-pleasing behaviors and struggle to assert boundaries. This is not weakness; it reflects their intense emotional attunement. Left unaddressed, it leads to burnout and pain.

The Trap of Emotional Debt

One of the most subtle and destructive lies empaths believe is this: If I give a little more, things will change. This belief creates what psychologists call emotional debt—a dynamic where the empath feels responsible for making the relationship work, regardless of cost. It sounds generous. In reality, it's exhausting.

In toxic relationships, emotional debt becomes a vicious cycle. The more the empath gives, the more is expected, and the less they receive in return. This imbalance breeds resentment, guilt, and confusion. The empath often blames themselves, thinking they haven't tried hard enough when, in fact, they've been giving too much for too long.

Scripture offers clarity in moments like these. In 2 Thessalonians 3:10, Paul writes, "The one who is unwilling to work shall not eat." While often applied to practical labor, this also speaks to emotional responsibility. When one person consistently carries another's emotional weight, growth is stunted on both sides. Enabling someone to avoid consequences is not love. Growth requires discomfort. Without it, change is nearly impossible.

When Empathy Becomes a Trap: A Fictional Story

Michael always saw his empathy as a strength. He was the one people turned to when life unraveled. When he met Sarah, her pain drew him like a magnet. She had endured betrayal, abandonment, and abuse. Michael felt compelled to be the one who wouldn't leave.

At first, their connection felt sacred. Sarah opened up, and Michael listened with compassion and patience. He told himself he was being Christlike—showing unconditional love she never received.

But slowly, the dynamic shifted. Sarah's need for reassurance became constant. Her gratitude faded, replaced by guilt trips and cold silences whenever Michael set limits. "After everything I've been through, how can you be so selfish?" she said. And Michael believed her.

He ignored his fatigue. Buried his needs. Told himself love meant sacrifice, and God would reward his faithfulness. But deep down, he felt himself slipping—emotionally drained and spiritually depleted. His prayers became desperate pleas: "God, what else do You want me to do?"

One evening, after yet another argument laced with blame and guilt, Michael sat alone with his Bible. His eyes fell on Mark 12:31: "Love your neighbor as yourself." For the first time, the second half pierced his heart.

As yourself.

Not instead of yourself. Not in place of yourself. As. Simultaneously.

At that moment, Michael realized he had been loving others more than he loved himself—and calling it righteousness. But God wasn't asking him to disappear for someone else's comfort. He was asking him to stand in truth and love—with strength, not surrender.

The shift didn't happen overnight. But little by little, Michael began to speak up. He stopped apologizing for boundaries. Released the belief that his love could save someone who didn't want to change. And with time, he rediscovered something he hadn't felt in years: peace.

Reflection Question

Have you ever felt emotionally responsible for someone else's healing or happiness? What beliefs kept you in that role? What might be different if you supported them but allowed them to take responsibility for themselves?

Final Thought

Empathy is a gift. But when you allow it to erase your needs, it becomes bondage. Genuine compassion respects the dignity of both people in a relationship. It allows others to face their own growth without interference and frees you to pursue well-being.

Jesus didn't call us to bleed endlessly for others. He already did that. He calls us to love with wisdom—compassion, courage, and clarity. You were never meant to disappear inside someone else's pain. Your voice, your peace, your boundaries—they matter too.

Caught in the Toxic Dance: Narcissists and Empaths

By now, we've followed the trail of pain back to its origins—childhood, where we first learned to survive instead of thrive. We didn't choose our circumstances, but we adapted. The roles we played, the defenses we built, and the people we were drawn to all made sense in light of what we were trying to protect. We entered what I call the Toxic Dance—a pattern shaped by survival and reinforced by familiar roles.

One of the most common pairings in this dance is the empath and the narcissist—not always as fixed identities, but as relational roles. Both may carry narcissistic tendencies, yet one leans into control and self-protection while the other leans into appeasement and caretaking. The one playing the narcissistic role craves admiration and influence. The one playing the empathic role seeks connection by rescuing and being needed.

It seems unlikely, but the pull is powerful. Unhealed wounds and unmet needs fuel the connection with an intensity that feels like love. Both are searching for love in the only way they've ever known—and both are left empty in the process.

These patterns weren't obvious. They were familiar. And the longer we stay in roles shaped by childhood pain, the more stuck we become. Psychology affirms this: we're wired to form protective patterns, even if those patterns begin to harm us. Scripture mirrors this reality: "There is a way that appears to be right, but in the end it leads to death" (Proverbs 14:12, NIV). What once protected us can become a prison.

Ignored Boundaries: A Fictional Story

A young woman from a broken family had been doing the hard work of healing. For years, two kinds of conditional love—romantic and brotherly—shaped her relationships. They were the only kinds she had ever known, and for a long time, they seemed like enough.

But now, she was ready for more. To move forward, she would have to release the comfort of the familiar and step into something more vulnerable.

Her sense of self was growing stronger. She began recognizing patterns instead of repeating them. Encouraged by her growth, she reached out to people she had hurt, hoping to rebuild trust.

But as those relationships resumed, so did the patterns. Without fully realizing it, she controlled conversations, reacted with emotional intensity, and assigned blame when misunderstood.

The people she contacted noticed. But this time, they didn't step back into the dance. They held firm to healthy boundaries. They chose not to enable what no longer aligned with healing.

To her, those boundaries felt like rejection.

She told herself they didn't care. That they were walking away. But in truth, they were loving her well, refusing to participate in a pattern that had once harmed her.

Feeling hurt and alone, she returned to the relationship she had finally left behind. The narcissist welcomed her back with charm and promises. He seemed softer, more open, willing to change.

She wanted to believe it.

For a moment, it felt like home. But the old dynamics soon returned. Charm gave way to criticism. Control resurfaced. And everything she had worked so hard to let go of came rushing back. Because what hadn't changed wasn't just him—it was the lie she was still believing.

Then it hit her like a familiar ache in a reopened wound.

She wasn't healing. She was in captivity again. She had walked out with hope but reentered through a revolving door. And that door, though wide open, disguised itself as restoration.

A False Choice, a Hidden Doorway

Is the toxicity ever escapable if we keep thinking like the child who believed they had to choose between love and security, but never both?

That old binary may have helped us survive, but it was never the whole truth. It's a Hobson's choice—a false dilemma disguised as freedom. Either way, we're stuck. We cling to control or caretaking, trying to feel safe. We find meaning in roles that once protected us. We become more skillful—but not freer.

What if real healing doesn't come from perfecting a broken strategy, but from rejecting the lie at its root? What if the path forward begins the moment we dare to say: I no longer accept the lie that I must choose between love and security—because God never asked me to.

Reflection Question

Have you ever returned to a familiar pattern, hoping it would be different, only to find yourself in the same pain again? Are you ready to accept that love and security are not a binary choice?

Final Thought

Control and unbridled empathy are the toxic dance. We speed it up, slow it down, change partners every year—but we're still stuck.

Until we recognize the false premise, nothing changes.

Empathy was never meant to drown you. It was meant to be a bridge—a way to feel deeply without losing yourself. Jesus already carried the heaviest load, so you no longer have to. He calls you to love with wisdom, not fear; with courage, not appeasement. Your voice, your peace, your boundaries—they matter, too.

But even with clarity, many of us still cling to old survival strategies. We keep trying to hold everyone else together—until our own bodies, minds, and souls whisper, "Enough."

In the next chapter, we'll uncover what happens; sensitivity and self-sacrifice aren't just costly emotionally, but physically. You'll see why the patterns that once kept you safe eventually turn against you—and how freedom begins when you reach the end of yourself.

6

Poetic Reflection of Part 1: Moving Beyond the Dance

We pause here, in the quiet ache of recognition.
How many times have we circled the same path,
hoping this time would feel different?
How often have we mistaken captivity for comfort?
The dance feels endless.

The roles, so familiar, seem like fate.
But pain is not destiny.

There is another rhythm
one that doesn't demand performance
or disguise itself as love.

It waits beyond the noise, patient and steady.
The doorway is still there.
And it's still open.

Let's keep walking together.

7

Part 2: When Coping Isn't Enough

Reaching the Limits of Survival Strategies

The toxic dance is exhausting.

By now, we've begun to name the patterns that shaped us—the caretaking, the control, and the invisible contracts we signed long before we even knew we had options. We didn't choreograph these moves consciously. We learned them early, practiced them often, and performed them well.

But what happens when the music keeps playing, and your body just wants to sit down? What happens when survival no longer feels like living?

This part of the journey isn't about blame or self-punishment. It's about recognizing the quiet cost of what once helped you get through. For many, the toxic dance isn't dramatic or violent, though it can be. It's subtle, familiar, and strangely safe. It can even feel like love. But deep down, something aches.

Maybe you've tried to fix the dance—changing partners, tempo, or steps—only to find yourself circling the same pain. Maybe you've told yourself, "This is just who I am," when really, it's who you had to become. Maybe you've carried the weight so long that setting it down feels unnatural, even dangerous.

Part 2 is where we gently, yet honestly, explore those costs and psychology's solutions. We'll look at what happens when the body begins to break under emotional strain. When the mind grows foggy from over-adapting. When relationships start to feel hollow. When authenticity is traded away for acceptance, or silence masquerades as peace. Maybe this isn't you, but it's still a danger you may be flirting with.

This section is about listening to your story, your symptoms, and your limits. It's about realizing that survival is not the same as healing, love, or safety. Whether you see yourself more as the narcissist, the empath, or somewhere in between, the question isn't who to blame. The real question is: What has this strategy cost you?

You've done what you had to do. And it worked—for a time. But now, the invitation is to examine whether those same strategies are still effective or if they're just keeping you stuck. There's no shame here. Only honesty. And maybe, for the first time, hope.

Imagine carrying an invisible weight—so familiar you barely notice it, yet heavy enough to drag your spirit down day after day. This weight is the cost of survival strategies learned in childhood, now hidden just beneath the surface of your daily life.

"There is a time for everything, a time to keep and a time to throw away" (Ecclesiastes 3:6, NIV). As you begin this next section, consider keeping a running list of how your body, relationships, and emotions may have been affected by your survival strategies. You don't need to fix anything yet. Just start noticing what your coping has cost.

Let's take a look at the price you've been paying—and whether it's time for a different kind of freedom.

8

Chapter 5: Revealing the Costs of Survival

Imagine carrying an invisible weight—one so familiar you barely notice it, yet heavy enough to drain your energy and dim your spirit day by day. This weight is the hidden toll of survival strategies learned early, quietly shaping your daily experience.

Endurance often comes at a price we don't fully recognize until we're overwhelmed. The fatigue, confusion, and emotional strain of navigating relationships shaped by narcissistic and empathic dynamics can quietly erode our sense of self. Welcome to life, right? Wrong. Coping gives us a moment to breathe, a way to steady ourselves so we don't collapse under the weight of our wounds. But coping isn't healing.

Many believe recovery is impossible because all they've ever known is how to manage pain—not how to remove its source.

This chapter reveals the consequences of toxic relationships and offers practical tools to ease the burden, reclaim your strength, and create space for true transformation. Coping helps us survive. Healing begins when we stop managing symptoms and begin confronting the roots.

Why You're Exhausted Despite Your Best Efforts

Endurance is wearing. Years spent navigating manipulation—managing control, absorbing emotions, and trying to keep everything stable—take a heavy toll. Emotional and mental fatigue isn't just tiredness.

Psychologists call this emotional burnout. Chronic stress overwhelms the mind and body, leaving no room for recovery before the next demand. When trapped in cycles of appeasement, hypervigilance, emotional suppression, or relentless strategizing, the nervous system stays locked in high alert. Prolonged stress floods the body with cortisol, fueling anxiety, memory issues, and physical ailments. Over time, even small tasks can feel impossible.

For many, these patterns evolve into Complex Post-Traumatic Stress Disorder (CPTSD), caused by prolonged relational trauma. Unlike acute PTSD, which stems from a single event, CPTSD develops gradually as the nervous system endures repeated overwhelm.

A hallmark of CPTSD is hypervigilance: a state of heightened alertness beyond simple anxiety. People living in it scan for danger, read between the lines, anticipate conflict, and brace for the next emotional blow. Genuine relaxation feels unsafe because the mind refuses to lower its guard.

Common Emotional and Mental Consequences

The unfortunate consequences of staying caught in these toxic relationships include:

- **Anxiety and Hypervigilance:** The need to anticipate reactions and avoid conflict keeps stress levels dangerously high. The physical sensation of hypervigilance can feel like your body parts are floating around because the brain area responsible for tracking your physical self-hunger, itch, pressure—has been redirected to threat monitoring.
- **Depression and Hopelessness:** Emotional depletion erodes motivation, leading to numbness, despair, and loss of purpose.

- **Emotional Numbness:** Suppressing feelings to survive manipulation leads to detachment. Joy and connection become harder to access.
- **Guilt and Shame:** Internalizing blame for toxic dynamics fosters unworthiness and self-doubt.
- **Cognitive Fog and Confusion:** Gaslighting and manipulation impair critical thinking, causing memory lapses and self-questioning.
- **Dissociation and Avoidance:** Mentally checking out or escaping into distraction is often the only way to cope.
- **Chronic Fatigue and Disrupted Sleep:** A nervous system stuck in survival mode sabotages rest. No amount of sleep seems to fix it.

Many survivors dissociate, numb emotions, or tighten control to create the illusion of safety. But the body knows, even when the mind tries to escape.

The Long Shadow of Childhood: The ACEs Study

For many, emotional depletion began in childhood. The Adverse Childhood Experiences (ACEs) study—a landmark research project on early trauma—found that adversity such as abuse, neglect, or dysfunction dramatically increases the risk of long-term emotional and physical harm. High ACE scores correlate with anxiety, depression, CPTSD, heart disease, diabetes, and autoimmune disorders. One staggering finding? A high ACE score can shorten life expectancy by up to 20 years.

I doubt any of us, as children, understood how deeply those early experiences would shape our futures. I didn't. Did you?

You can readily find this study, its findings, and even self-administer the test on the internet. As an action item, look into this further.

Depletion affects more than just you. Emotionally drained people may unintentionally hurt those around them. An overwhelmed heart struggles to love well. A depleted soul may withdraw or try to control. Though unintentional, the damage is real.

Recognizing this isn't just for yourself—it's also for those affected by your survival strategies.

A Call for Restoration

When we've been stuck in endurance mode too long, our bodies and minds eventually tell the truth. These signals aren't failures. They're evidence that it's time to step out of emergency mode.

For many, that shift feels impossible. Who will keep everything in order if I stop? Who will manage the chaos? The fear of letting go can be overwhelming.

As I began to consider what real restoration might look like, I came across a line of Scripture that stopped me in my tracks: "In repentance and rest is your salvation, in quietness and trust is your strength" (Isaiah 30:15, NIV). It's not striving. Not overworking. Not holding everything together. It's quietness. Trust. And the willingness to return.

That verse felt like permission to exhale. A reminder that deep strength doesn't come from control—it comes from surrender. Even under pressure, a more profound peace is waiting for us.

"Come to me, all you who are weary and burdened, and I will give you rest... For my yoke is easy and my burden is light" (Matthew 11:28, 30, NIV).

A Physical Toll: A Personal Story

When I first encountered the ACEs study, I calculated my score. The number shocked me. The survival strategies I had relied on since childhood helped me endure, but they also paved the way for long-term damage. My ACE score was seven, which statistically shortens life expectancy by two decades. I've already outlived that prediction. Good thing I started this journey of transformation when I did.

The emotional and mental impacts were obvious. But one physical consequence nearly crippled me: gout.

For those unfamiliar, gout is the accumulation of uric acid crystals in the joints, usually in the body's lowest points. These crystals work like sandpaper on open wounds every time the joint moves. For me, they settled in my big toe. The pain was indescribable. My joint swelled, grinding with every movement. For years, I genuinely believed amputation was my best option.

I couldn't walk. Sitting and standing were both excruciating. Twice a year, gout would strike and leave me bedridden flat on my back for four to six weeks. Some cases are dietary. Mine stemmed from unrelenting stress and anxiety.

I didn't just work from home—I worked from bed—on my back. When I had to move, I crawled to the bathroom with my foot elevated behind me.

Something had to change.

As I began the same journey toward healing that you are on now, things shifted. The attacks grew less intense. Then less frequent. Eventually, they stopped.

I have had one episode in years.

Reflection Question

What price have you paid for continuing to use the strategies you learned in childhood?

Final Thought

When we've been trapped in endurance mode too long, our bodies and minds begin to protest. Don't ignore the signals.

Track the emotional toll. Write it down. Name it.

Because that toll is your motive.

It's your why.

And your why may be the key to your breakthrough.

As we begin to uncover the emotional and mental costs, it's vital to turn our attention to the body—the physical keeper of these unspoken burdens. What happens when the strain no longer stays silent but demands to be felt and acknowledged?

When Your Body Says "Enough": The Physical Toll

As the emotional toll mounts, it often speaks loudly through the body. When the mind and heart can no longer carry the burden alone, the physical self begins to say, Enough. This profound language of the body is a universal yet deeply personal call for healing, one that Scripture and science both recognize as vital yet too often overlooked.

The pain you've been carrying—both emotional and physical—was never meant to be ignored. Chronic illness, exhaustion, and other symptoms are your vessel's way of urging you to pay attention.

Many of us have walked through emotional wounds, manipulation, or extended seasons of tension. But the body remembers like a vault that never forgets. The survival strategies that once served you as a child no longer protect you. The strain they stored didn't disappear—it settled deep within your nervous and immune systems, even down to your cells. Can you feel it?

The Mind-Body Connection: When Stress Speaks

The mind and body aren't strangers; they're in constant conversation. When emotional pain goes unspoken, grief is buried, and fear becomes baseline, the physical being reacts as if danger never ended—trapped in an endless survival loop. Pause for a moment—can you feel the echo of this in your own experience?

Hormones like cortisol and adrenaline, designed for short bursts of emergency, flood your system day after day. Over time, that flood drains resources. The immune defenses weaken. Inflammation rises. Sleep slips away. Digestion falters. Healing slows.

Your frame learns to live on high alert. Exhaustion becomes persistent fatigue, autoimmune flare-ups, fibromyalgia, migraines, and hormonal imbalances. These aren't random—they're your body's way of signaling, something isn't right.

Autoimmune conditions often arise where trauma remains unresolved, as if your system is turning on itself, echoing repressed anger, pain, and blame. Chronic fatigue syndrome is another example. It's not laziness or weakness—it's a body that has fled danger so long it finally collapses.

Cardiovascular issues. IBS. Acid reflux. Migraines. Chronic pain. Research is clear: long-term emotional distress is rarely just emotional. Our biology isn't designed to carry that weight indefinitely.

Even daily micro-stressors—dismissal, manipulation, invalidation—don't just bounce off. Your physical self doesn't distinguish between minor betrayals and major trauma. It accumulates both.

When tension becomes chronic, your brain struggles too. Imaging shows long-term strain impacts the prefrontal cortex and limbic system—areas tied to emotional regulation and decision-making. When your brain stays in survival mode, even basic self-care—showers, teeth brushing, healthy eating—feels like climbing a mountain. It's not a lack of will—it's neurobiology doing its best under pressure.

Unfortunately, many shame those who struggle instead of lifting them up, increasing stress and worsening situations. Not here. Here, we recognize truth and move in loving, positive directions, honoring the precious gift we often stand in the way of: ourselves.

Scripture and the Body's Voice

For those who draw from Scripture, the Bible speaks tenderly about the physical self. Paul writes, "Do you not know that your bodies are temples of the Holy Spirit, who is in you... Therefore, honor God with your bodies" (1 Corinthians 6:19–20, NIV).

This Scripture isn't offered as morality policing, health rules, or shame. It's about seeing your body as sacred and worthy of care—no matter your beliefs. To honor your body is to listen to it—to stop treating pain as inconvenience and begin treating it as meaningful communication.

Jesus said to His disciples, "Come with me by yourselves to a quiet place and get some rest" (Mark 6:31, NIV). Even the Son of God acknowledged that constant giving has a cost. Rest isn't indulgent—it's necessary.

The Weight That Would Not Leave

The ACE Study began in an obesity clinic led by Dr. Vincent Felitti. Patients lost weight—some hundreds of pounds—but many regained it quickly or dropped out. Not because they lacked discipline, but because the weight served a purpose.

When Felitti asked about childhood experiences, the truth emerged: abuse, neglect, abandonment. For many, their weight wasn't a problem; it was armor. It made them feel safer, less vulnerable, or more powerful. When the weight came off, they felt exposed. What hadn't healed still drove them.

This study transformed how many view obesity. For some, the issue isn't carbs or fats—it's a coping mechanism. Symptoms remain as long as the wound does.

Jeremiah reminds us, "But I will restore you to health and heal your wounds, declares the Lord" (Jeremiah 30:17, NIV). God doesn't start with the weight. He starts with the wounds.

The Power of Being Seen

Another ACE Study finding reveals something deeply human: patients given just one moment of compassion experienced lasting improvements. This is the power of Agape love at work.

After completing the ACE questionnaire, doctors offered a simple, compassionate response: "I see you've experienced difficult things as a child. These experiences are common and can affect health. If you want to talk, I'm here." No therapy required. No probing. Just acknowledgment and openness.

Dr. Felitti reported that trauma-informed care led to a 35% drop in medical visits and an 11% drop in hospitalizations over a year.

Agape love may sound soft—but it changes lives.

This recalls what my uncle did for me in the "Pumpkin Pie Story" from

Chapter 2. Decades later, internalizing his words, "He will stay with me," helped heal my CPTSD. That expression of Agape love was transformative.

Proverbs says, "Gracious words are a honeycomb, sweet to the soul and healing to the bones" (Proverbs 16:24, NIV). Validation isn't extra. It's essential. When you feel seen, you begin to see yourself differently.

If you, the reader, haven't figured it out yet, hear this: "I see you, I know you and you matter to me."

Reflection Question

Who could you extend a compassionate, Dr. Felitti-style response to—someone who needs to hear, "I understand your struggles, and I'm here to talk?" Who might benefit from gentler care or lowered medical bills?

Practical Self-Care Invitation

Begin tracking your health challenges—physical, emotional, and mental—as you progress through this book. Note any changes, big or small, in symptoms, energy, or well-being. Journaling these shifts will help you witness your body's voice and the impact of healing beyond survival. If you feel comfortable, consider sharing these insights with someone you trust; healing often grows in connection.

Final Thought

Healing begins with living in love—and letting love in. Your body isn't broken. It's been loyal. And now, it's asking for rest, safety, and truth. Like a worn but steadfast compass, it points the way home.

Losing Yourself to Safety

The last section showed how the body says enough when survival demands too much. But survival doesn't just shape your health—it reshapes your very sense of self.

A genuine self struggles under the weight of performance or the constant need for external approval. It withers when life becomes a stage instead of a home. But it flourishes when rooted in purpose, real connection, and emotional freedom. Lives aligned with their deepest design overflow with "the fruits of the Spirit: love, joy, peace, forbearance, kindness, goodness, faithfulness, gentleness, and self-control" (Galatians 5:22–23, NIV). Those who embrace their honest selves often show remarkable resilience. They laugh easily. They care deeply without manipulation or fear.

This isn't just philosophy. Psychology affirms that emotional well-being thrives when we live in alignment with who we truly are.

Carl Rogers, a pioneer of humanistic psychology, taught that people grow best when their self-concept reflects lived experience rather than a mask imposed by others. When we live congruently, fulfillment and growth flow naturally, lifting the heavy weight of false selves we once believed we had to carry.

Yet this wisdom didn't begin in the 20th century. Long before psychology named it, Jesus revealed that real life doesn't come from constructing safer versions of ourselves but from surrendering them entirely. His words aren't merely insight—they are the foundation that every other insight only echoes.

"For whoever wants to save their life will lose it, but whoever loses their life for me will find it" (Matthew 16:25, NIV). Here lies a profound truth: when we cling to self-made identities, crafted from fear and self-preservation, we lose sight of who we really are. But when we release those constructs and root ourselves in grace and love, we rediscover a life that is free, grounded, and whole.

The Identity Collapse

Early coping mechanisms meant to secure love or safety can quietly harden into identity. Through control, compliance, or avoidance, these patterns replace honesty with roles that may be easier to perform but harder to live within.

Eventually, we become strangers to our own design, shaped not by truth but by what we believed we had to be to make it through.

How Empaths Lose Their Selves

For many empaths, love becomes tangled with self-erasure. But love isn't about giving until nothing remains; it's about giving from wholeness. Even Jesus, the embodiment of sacrificial care, set boundaries. "When a crowd tried to push Him off a cliff, He simply walked right through the crowd and went on his way" (Luke 4:30, NIV). His love was pure and self-giving, but never self-negating.

Love rooted in wisdom requires a grounded self—someone who knows their worth and honors their limits. Without boundaries, empaths risk enabling dysfunction rather than embodying Agape.

Pause and ask yourself: how would you draw loving boundaries?

How Narcissists Lose Themselves

Narcissists, by contrast, protect their inner vulnerability by constructing a false self—an idealized image built to secure admiration and avoid shame. Control and dominance become substitutes for intimacy. Over time, this façade feels more real than the person beneath it. The larger the gap between their public image and private emptiness, the more isolated they feel—even in the spotlight.

Whether it's the empaths' people-pleasing or the narcissists' perfectionism, both paths originate in self-preservation. The empath becomes what others want. The narcissist becomes what feels safest. Yet neither path leads to lasting peace. Both lose something precious along the way—the honest, God-given self.

Scripture affirms this truth: "For we are God's workmanship, created in Christ Jesus to do good works, which God prepared in advance for us to do" (Ephesians 2:10, NIV). Your truest self isn't something you invent—it's someone you were lovingly designed to be. Healing isn't just returning to yourself; it's returning to the you that was intended from the beginning.

Claire's Journey Toward Rediscovery: A Fictional Story

Claire had always been the dependable one. Family, friends, and coworkers leaned on her strength, and she gave it freely. But she was running on empty. Somewhere along the way, her own needs slipped from view. She'd mistaken self-sacrifice for love.

One evening, when a close friend asked for yet another favor, Claire agreed, as always. But afterward, a wave of weariness washed over her. She hadn't checked in with her heart. She realized her identity had become so wrapped up in meeting others' needs that her own had disappeared.

In that moment, something shifted. Claire saw clearly: this wasn't love. This was losing herself.

A phrase echoed in her spirit: True care flows from fullness, not depletion. Even Jesus rested. Even He walked away when necessary.

Claire began practicing small, brave acts of boundary-setting and self-compassion. It felt awkward, tinged with guilt and doubt. But she also felt something unfamiliar: a growing peace.

Gradually, the person she once was began to reawaken. And with her came the kind of love that doesn't break you down but builds you up.

Reflection Question

How has your search for safety shaped your identity? Who do you believe you are today, and who do you long to become?

Practical Exercise

Over the next week, notice moments when you slip into old coping patterns—whether it looks like people-pleasing, controlling, avoiding, or seeking approval. For each moment, journal how it affected your sense of self beneath those roles.

Then choose one small, specific step toward expressing your genuine self—perhaps setting a healthy boundary, practicing honest self-compassion, or asking for support without fear. Try this step once, and note how it feels both during and after.

Final Thought

Healing is coming home to the person you were always meant to be. You were never meant to disappear in order to be loved. In reclaiming your voice, your worth, and your truth, you rediscover not just who you are but the kind of love that truly sets you free.

The Price of Pretending

Sometimes, without realizing it, we focus so much on meeting expectations that we drift far from our real selves. Outwardly, we're functioning. Helpful. Even successful. But this is not who we are.

What we often don't see is that survival frequently requires hiding.

Preferences are tucked away to keep the peace. Opinions are edited down to stay likable. Needs are muted so they won't feel too much. Over time, the costumed version of ourselves starts to feel like the only one others will accept. So we shrink. We shape-shift. We act the part.

We call it maturity, responsibility, even wisdom. But so often, it's just fear wearing a clever disguise.

Scripture names this quiet loss: "What good is it for someone to gain the whole world, yet forfeit their soul?" (Mark 8:36, NIV). This verse isn't only about material success. It speaks to anything we chase at the expense of our unedited self. We can gain approval, admiration—even affection—yet lose the essence of who we were created to be.

The toll is steep.

Relationships grow shallow, stripped of the intimacy only truth can bring. Decisions become paralyzing when we've trained ourselves to prioritize everyone else's needs before our own. Life turns into a well-rehearsed script, impressive outside and hollow inside. Peace is missing. Purpose slips away. And we tell ourselves we're fine.

I once heard someone say, "I used to think I was free because I wasn't fighting anyone. But I realized I wasn't free. I was just silent." That silence—the absence of your voice, your dreams, and your needs—isn't peace. It's erasure.

The Shift: A Fictional Story

Jasmine was known for being reliable. At work, she was the go-to person. Always prepared, always agreeable. In friendships, she listened more than she spoke. In her marriage, she minimized her needs, believing it was the selfless thing to do.

People liked her. They often said so.

Inside, Jasmine felt invisible. She existed within the outline of a person everyone admired but no one truly knew.

The turning point came one quiet evening as she was cleaning the kitchen, music humming in the background. Out of nowhere, a childhood memory surfaced: sitting by a window, painting watercolors. She remembered how alive she felt. Creative. Unafraid. Back then, there was no one to impress—only color, movement, and joy.

That weekend, she bought a small set of paints. Just for fun, she told herself. She hadn't painted in years, but as she dipped her brush into the colors, something stirred. It wasn't just creativity. It was her. A part of herself she hadn't been in a long time. Each brushstroke felt like an act of remembrance.

Jasmine didn't blow up her life. She didn't quit her job or confront everyone she knew. But she began to say no. She stopped apologizing for needing space. She signed up for an art class. She started asking herself what she wanted before asking what others needed. Gradually, her world felt less like a performance and more like a homecoming.

Action Step

Write yourself a receipt. At the top, title it "Recurring Bill from the Toxic Dance." List the emotional, relational, and physical toll you've paid to maintain the strategy you adopted in childhood—whether it's people-pleasing, perfectionism, silence, or control. Be honest. Include what it costs you in joy, rest, connection, relationships, or health.

At the bottom, write "Paid" and today's date. Sign it.

Reflection Question

Are you ready for some serious bill reductions? Do you have your motivation—and your reason—to look for a better strategy than the one you learned as a child?

Final Thought

The mask you've worn is not your authentic self. You were designed to live whole and unedited, not shaped by fear. Returning to who you were meant to be is the first step to a love that truly sets you free.

As we look ahead to Chapter 6, it's important to hold this truth: psychological tools, while valuable, can only take us so far. True transformation requires moving beyond managing symptoms to addressing the deep roots of our pain.

Together, we will explore both the strengths and the limits of psychology—and discover how Scripture's truth invites us into lasting freedom. The healing lessons in Scripture are for everyone, believers and skeptics alike. Faith is not a requirement to receive.

9

Chapter 6: Exploring the Limits of Psychology

We all carry wounds from childhood—deep needs for love and security that shaped how we cope today. These early survival strategies helped us get through the hardest moments, but what if they're no longer enough? What if, instead of healing, they keep us stuck in a toxic dance—polishing the pain without ever setting us free?

Psychology offers tools that ease the pain and bring clarity. But are they enough to reach the roots where true healing begins? Let's take an honest look at what modern therapy can do—and where it falls short.

Modern therapies can bring real relief. They offer clarity, support, and tools to manage overwhelming thoughts and emotions. They're a good beginning.

But here's the question worth pausing on: Do these tools truly heal the roots? Or do they simply polish the costume while we keep dancing to the same music? Let's look honestly at what these tools can do—and where they fall short.

Rewiring Thoughts: Helpful, but Not Enough

Our minds buzz with countless thoughts every day. Some lift us up. Others weigh us down. Cognitive Behavioral Therapy (CBT) is one of the most widely used approaches today. It rests on a simple but powerful truth: our thoughts shape our feelings, and our feelings shape our actions.

When pain and fear twist our thinking, we start seeing ourselves and the world through a distorted lens. CBT helps us notice those distortions. It invites us to ask:

- Is this thought really true?
- If it's not, what else might be true?

For those carrying deep emotional wounds, some thoughts can feel like stone walls:

- Maybe it was all my fault.
- I always end up hurt.
- No one really stays. These aren't fleeting thoughts. They're scripts etched deep within us—designed to keep us safe, but they also keep us stuck.

Maybe you've tried pushing back on them—challenging, reframing, repeating affirmations and yet you still feel the weight. That isn't failure. It's your soul whispering, "There's more here." Look closer.

CBT can guide us toward truth, but it's not the final destination. It's a path you choose again and again. Scripture echoes the same invitation: "Finally, brothers and sisters, whatever is true, think about such things" (Philippians 4:8, NIV).

Reframing: Making Space for a New Perspective

One of CBT's gifts is reframing—stepping back to see painful experiences in a wider frame. Not to dismiss the pain, but to place it in a bigger story:

- A mistake doesn't make you worthless.
- Rejection doesn't mean you're unlovable.
- An ending isn't the end of you.

Reframing doesn't erase facts. It reshapes the meaning we give them.

Still, I know how hard it is to loosen your grip on an old story when it feels like the only net you have. I've resisted new perspectives too, holding tight because letting go felt like falling.

The Birthday That Changed Everything: A Fictional Story

Marissa dreaded her birthday. As a child, it marked her father's absence and conflict. As an adult, she told herself it didn't matter. But inside, her heart clenched.

That morning, the kitchen felt cold. The faint hum of the fridge was the only sound as she sat on the hard tile floor. Tears slipped down her cheeks, quiet and steady. Her breath came in shallow bursts, each sob an unspoken admission of the loneliness she carried deep inside.

I'm not worth celebrating, she whispered.

Later, her phone rang. It was Kate, surprised Marissa hadn't mentioned her birthday.

When Marissa finally shared her pain, Kate listened without judgment and said softly, Maybe they just didn't know how much it mattered to you.

That didn't erase the hurt. But it opened a small crack.

Marissa began to wonder: What if my birthday isn't cursed? What if I've been protecting myself too much? What if next year, I let others know what I need?

Her past didn't change. But her future began to open.

Narrative Therapy: Choosing a Better Story

We all carry stories about who we are and what life holds. Narrative therapy asks: Is the story I'm telling helping me move forward—or holding me back? It reminds us: the story isn't finished. You still hold the pen.

I've looked at my own life and realized I was still living someone else's script—one written in fear and survival. That realization stung, but it freed me to begin rewriting.

Paul's life shows this same power. Once a persecutor, he became a healer. Romans 12:2 urges us: "Be transformed by the renewing of your mind." (NIV)

These cognitive tools help begin that renewal—not by denial, but by re-authoring.

Behavioral Activation: Doing Before You Feel Ready

Sometimes the bravest step is simply to move.

Behavioral activation encourages small actions—making the bed, taking a walk, calling a friend. They seem ordinary, but they send a loud message: I'm still here. I'm moving forward.

Movement doesn't always feel magical, but it breaks the stillness that pain tries to trap us in. James 2:17 reminds us: "Faith by itself, if it is not accompanied by action, is dead." (NIV)

An Assumed Anchor: Truth

Here's what often gets missed in psychological tools: the new picture must be grounded in truth.

Reframing only helps if it leans into what's real. Comfortable lies might soothe for a moment, but they fracture us in other ways. Gaslighting yourself is still gaslighting.

In a world where truth bends to preference, this is hard to hear. Healing can't grow from illusions. It has to be anchored in reality—the kind that sets us free, even if it shakes us, even if it humbles us, even if it calls us to change.

I know how tempting comforting lies can be. I've clung to them myself. But truth doesn't shame. It steadies. It restores. The Bible warns: "They perish because they refused to love the truth and so be saved" (2 Thessalonians 2:10, NIV). We're not just called to know the truth, but to love it—even when it costs us comfort, security, or our old stories.

Psychology is only now catching up to what Scripture has whispered all along: truth doesn't just feel better—it sets you free.

Reflection Question

When you listen to your thoughts, where might shifting their meaning open space for hope or growth?

Action Step

Notice one recurring negative thought today. Write it down. Then ask yourself: Did the person or event that triggered this actually say it—or is it how I interpreted the situation? What is something more truthful and life-giving I can hold onto instead?

Final Thought

Psychology offers helpful tools. They can begin the climb out of the hole. But step by step, it's truth that lights the way forward.

But even truth, when it's only in our minds, can feel distant. To truly heal, it must move from head to heart—and that's where psychology begins to meet its limits.

Emotional Mastery: Why Managing Isn't Healing

In the last section, we explored how reframing and rewiring thoughts can shift the stories we tell ourselves. But what about emotions—the ones that ambush you without warning?

Lena stared at her phone, her heart pounding as if running from something unseen. One message. Just one line. And her peace was shattered.

She told herself it wasn't a big deal. People text like that all the time. But an old signal tightened in her chest, firm and unrelenting. She felt the familiar cocktail: panic, confusion, and shame rising like a tide she couldn't stop. Had she misunderstood? Overreacted? Or was she finally learning to recognize manipulation for what it was?

This is where emotional regulation begins—listening to your feelings without letting them take the wheel.

Why Emotional Regulation Matters

Emotional regulation is the ability to experience emotions without being ruled by them. It's the difference between reacting and responding. In unhealthy relationships—especially manipulative ones—emotions often drive the entire dynamic. One person uses guilt, shame, or fear to control, and the other gets trapped trying to manage both their own emotions and someone else's.

But regulation isn't suppression. It's not pretending you don't feel what you feel. It's creating enough inner space to respond with wisdom. That's how you reclaim agency and protect your peace.

The Bible reminds us: "A person without self-control is like a city with broken-down walls" (Proverbs 25:28, NIV). Emotional regulation rebuilds those walls—not to shut people out, but to safeguard what's within.

The Role of Awareness

You cannot regulate what you refuse to recognize. Many of us learned early to minimize our feelings just to survive. We brushed off discomfort, downplayed pain, or told ourselves, It's not that bad. I'm fine.

But emotions aren't the enemy. They're messengers.

Anger might signal a boundary crossed. Anxiety might point to old wounds resurfacing. When you notice and name what you feel—even clumsily—you stop drowning in it and begin observing it with clarity.

That knot in your stomach? Those racing thoughts? Pause. Name what's happening. This kind of awareness is a quiet act of grace toward yourself. It says, I'm willing to meet myself here, without judgment.

Tools That Help

When emotions flare, the right tools can bring you back to center:

- **Grounding:** Plant your feet firmly on the floor. Notice five things you can see. Feel the chair beneath you. This simple act pulls your attention back to the present moment.
- **Breathwork:** Inhale deeply for four counts, hold for four, exhale slowly for six. This signals your nervous system that you're safe.
- **Journaling:** Write freely about what you're feeling. Untangling thoughts on paper often untangles them in your mind.
- **Scripture and Meditation:** Reflect on verses that bring peace. "Be still, and know that I am God" (Psalm 46:10, NIV) can steady a restless heart.

These practices calm the storm. They help you pause. They help you survive. But they're stopgaps. They don't reach the roots—and real growth always starts there. Later chapters will go deeper, beyond self-management into restoration.

When Emotions Get Hijacked

Sometimes emotions don't just arrive—they crash over you like a wave you never saw coming. One moment you're steady. The next, you're yelling, withdrawing, or retreating into the familiar shadows of shame.

When that happens, don't rush to self-judgment. Pause. Take a breath. Ask yourself gently, What just felt threatened? What is my heart trying to protect?

That simple curiosity can uncover triggers you didn't know were there—threads that tie back to old wounds and familiar fears. And with each glimpse of understanding, you give yourself a little more space to choose differently next time.

Paul reminds us: "Do not be overcome by evil, but overcome evil with good" (Romans 12:21, NIV). Overcoming with good isn't about pretending everything's fine. It's about pausing long enough to choose wisdom over impulse—even if wisdom, in that moment, is as small and sacred as simply waiting before you act.

Rebuilding Your Inner World

Learning to regulate your emotions is like renovating a house that's been neglected for years. At first, it feels overwhelming—dust everywhere, broken pieces you're not sure how to fix. But slowly, as you clear the clutter, light begins to seep in.

With that clarity comes courage. The courage to say, This feels wrong, or I need space, even when others disapprove. The courage to stop letting guilt, manipulation, or silence dictate your every move.

Regulation breaks the old cycle where your feelings were used against you. And most importantly, it helps you hear your own voice again—stronger, steadier, and kinder than you remembered.

If your past taught you to bury your emotions just to survive, this is how you begin to unlearn that habit. And in the quiet, if you listen closely, you may hear a still, small voice whispering: You matter. Your peace matters.

The Limits of Psychology

Breathwork, grounding, and journaling can be powerful tools. They create space between stimulus and response, helping you move through emotional storms with steadier hands.

Psychology teaches the value of managing emotions—and Scripture agrees: "Fools give full vent to their rage, but the wise bring calm in the end" (Proverbs 29:11, NIV). Emotional maturity means managing your inner world rather than letting it master you.

But even after we do our best—pausing, breathing, writing—the storm sometimes lingers. And this is where psychology reaches its edge. It equips us to carry the burden well, but it doesn't restore us to who we were designed to be.

The Bible goes further: "Cast all your anxiety on Him because He cares for you" (1 Peter 5:7, NIV). Emotional strength doesn't mean you never struggle. It means you know where to go when you do. "And the peace of God, which transcends all understanding, will guard your hearts and your minds in Christ Jesus" (Philippians 4:7, NIV).

Psychology often stops where Scripture begins. It can't yet explain how a hardened heart—even one trapped in narcissistic rage—can soften. The Bible does. In the next part of this book, we'll explore how grace reaches even the places psychology calls incurable.

Reflection Question

When emotions rise, do you pause to understand their source—or do you react? Which has brought you closer to peace?

A Final Thought

Emotional mastery means showing up for yourself when feelings are loud and unfiltered. It's listening without surrendering, responding without retreating, and moving forward without letting emotions take the wheel.

Physiological Coping: Physical and Chemical Life Support

Have you ever felt your heart pounding uncontrollably, your body flooded with anxious energy, or suddenly gone numb? These aren't just fleeting feelings or mental whispers—they're your body's urgent signals demanding to be heard.

In those moments, your physiology does exactly what it was designed to do: protect you. But sometimes, it takes over completely. Without understanding this, it's easy to mistake temporary relief for lasting change.

Let's explore what physical and chemical life support really means.

Most people think of life support as machines in a hospital—ventilators, IVs, sedatives. It's a fitting metaphor. When a body can't function on its own, it needs external help just to survive. Many of us live this way too—walking around seeming fine but leaning on substances or coping strategies just to keep going. Psychology often plays this role as well.

The Body in Survival Mode

When your body is trapped in survival mode, like a car stuck in first gear, growth and connection stall, and safety becomes a single, relentless pursuit. Trauma, chronic stress, and emotional neglect aren't just mental struggles—they're experiences that affect your whole body.

Your brain senses danger and floods your system with stress hormones like cortisol and adrenaline. Blood pressure rises. Digestion slows. Muscles tense. Breathing becomes shallow. It wears you down. It disconnects you. Over time, this state of constant alertness becomes your new normal—but it steals your vitality and your peace.

No wonder you reach for relief. Your body craves comfort—not just pleasure, but survival. Yet most comforts don't heal.

Modern Entrapments

Today's world offers endless ways to soothe an overwhelmed system:

- Streaming distractions
- Sugary snacks
- Social media scrolling
- Pornography
- Pills
- Performance pressure

These are all forms of physical or chemical life support—quick fixes that regulate distress but don't restore wholeness.

They have one thing in common: they replace real connection with imitation. Stimulation instead of intimacy. Sedation instead of comfort. Escape instead of transformation.

Psychology's Role—and Its Limits

Psychology recognizes this exhausting cycle, offering breathwork, grounding exercises, trauma-informed therapies, and medications that can lighten the load when the body feels overwhelmed.

For many, these tools are lifelines. But when they become permanent solutions rather than temporary support, they risk imitating peace instead of cultivating it.

Sometimes, the coping shifts from one crutch to another. The outside may change, but the inner ache remains.

The Spiritual Reality Psychology Can't Fully Address

What happens if we dull the pain but leave the root cause untouched? Calm the body but starve the soul? Choose love without security, or security without love?

Psychology focuses heavily on biology—chemical imbalances, overactive amygdalae, nervous system dysregulation—addressing symptoms but not the deeper spiritual need.

Psalm 23 doesn't promise, "He adjusts my neurotransmitters." Instead, it declares, "He restores my soul."

Jesus healed the sick and calmed storms inside and out. But more than that, He restored people to relationship, love, and truth. He went beneath the surface to heal what really mattered.

That's something psychology alone can't fully offer. It may quiet your coping system, but it can't replace it. It can lessen pain but not renew the spirit.

Without true connection, coping tools only imitate peace. Biblical peace is more than the absence of distress—it's the presence of wholeness.

Where Do We Go From Here?

This isn't a critique of therapy, medication, or coping mechanisms—they're often essential. But honesty about their limits is vital.

They are tools—not destinations.

Your body matters. Your chemistry matters. But if we stop there, we're living on life support, never fully alive. There is a way off the machines, but it requires more than management. It requires restoration.

Reflection Question

What forms of life support do you lean on—physical, chemical, emotional, or other modern escapes? Are you noticing how treating symptoms without addressing root causes keeps you stuck?

Final Thought

You weren't made to merely survive on life support. The world offers sedation and quick fixes. Psychology offers valuable insight—but the Bible speaks straight to the heart of the soul's deepest restoration.

Let your body rest—but don't let it lead. Healing begins where life truly does—not in the chemistry, but in the soul.

And the best news? This healing is available to everyone, whether or not you believe in God.

Coping vs. Living: Choosing Roots that Bear Fruit

"It's time to move beyond the toxic dance,
because survival isn't living."

From the very beginning, every human shares a profound and urgent need for two essentials: love and security. As children, this need often feels so pressing that we unconsciously choose between them. That early choice made in moments of vulnerability and confusion sets the stage for how we learn to navigate life.

Psychology honors these survival strategies, recognizing them as our best efforts to adapt. It focuses on refining these tools, polishing the habits that helped us endure. Yet this approach assumes the childhood choice was the best we could have made. It assumes survival was enough.

When Coping Becomes a Cage

Coping strategies are like shields and swords. They protect us and fend off threats. They guard us from pain, fear, and rejection. But while they keep us alive, they can also trap us in patterns that are confining, exhausting, and ultimately unfulfilling.

Imagine trying to live your whole life wearing armor designed for battle. The protection comes at a cost: heaviness, restriction, and distance from real connection. Coping strategies, no matter how skillfully honed, are survival tools—not life-giving foundations. They mask pain but don't remove it. They manage symptoms but don't heal the cause.

What helped us survive often won't help us heal.

In a culture that celebrates self-sufficiency, hustle, and hyper-independence, it's easy to mistake exhaustion for strength—and isolation for wisdom. These messages reinforce the illusion that we can protect ourselves into peace.

But peace doesn't come from better armor. It comes from walking the narrow path.

Roots Run Deep

To understand why coping falls short, we must look beneath the surface—to the source from which our behaviors grow. Actions, attitudes, and feelings are the fruits of those roots. Good roots produce nourishing fruit, but surface polishing won't yield healthy outcomes if pain, fear, or unmet needs still entangle the foundation.

The roots that sustain our coping often carry the scars of childhood: rejection, neglect, fear, and confusion. These roots run deep and shape everything we do, often without our awareness. Until we transform them, our behaviors and emotional patterns will reflect survival, not true life.

A Quiet Pause for Reflection

Think back gently, without judgment, to moments when you felt forced to choose. Did you cling to love, even when it wasn't safe? Or did you settle for security, even if it meant love felt out of reach? Those choices made sense then. They protected you when you had no other options. But those same decisions may still quietly shape how you relate to yourself and others today.

What would it mean to stop letting those old moments decide the health of your present relationships?

The Earthquake Beneath: Shifting from Surviving to Thriving

Here is the tectonic shift: moving from a life of coping to one rooted in transformation. It's not about trying harder or perfecting old strategies. It's about planting new foundations—ones that yield new life. The shift is from relationships built on fears to relationships built on love.

It is a seismic realignment of how we experience ourselves, others, and, if you are ready, God.

Reading the Fruits: What Your Life Reveals

The apostle Paul gives us a vivid picture of two very different lives in his letter to the Galatians. First, he names the acts born of fear, survival, and separation: "The acts of the flesh are obvious: sexual immorality, impurity and debauchery; idolatry and witchcraft; hatred, discord, jealousy, fits of rage, selfish ambition, dissensions, factions and envy; drunkenness, orgies, and the like" (Galatians 5:19–21, NIV).

What strikes me in this list is the amount of unresolved and unnecessary pain, and I hope you see it too. Look at the lack of connection and true intimacy. Shifting away from the fear-based system we adopted as a child to a love-based relationship system we can choose at any time removes these problems much more easily than white knuckling. Healing is not about exerting more control over broken systems, but replacing the system itself.

These are not simply moral failings. They are often expressions of coping—a divided heart trying to hold love and security apart, settling for less, and causing harm along the way.

In contrast, Paul lists the fruit of the Spirit: "But the fruit of the Spirit is love, joy, peace, forbearance, kindness, goodness, faithfulness, gentleness, and self-control" (Galatians 5:22–23, NIV). Connection. Intimacy. These qualities flow from foundations nourished by grace, forgiveness, and unconditional love. They reflect the life we were created to live—where love and security exist in harmony.

Grace: The Unseen Shield

Grace is the first root of new life. It is unearned, unconditional, and freely given. Grace becomes both a shield and a gift. It protects us from bitterness, resentment, and the exhausting need to earn love or defend ourselves from rejection.

Think of grace as an invisible covering that doesn't weigh you down but lifts you up. It allows you to release old wounds—not by denying them, but by replacing their power with something greater: acceptance and peace.

Forgiveness: Clearing the Toxic Ground

Forgiveness is the cleansing rain that softens hardened soil. It releases the toxic grip of the past so wounds no longer poison the present. Forgiveness, rooted in grace, makes the ground fertile again.

It clears the way for new life to grow.

Love: The Welcoming Mat

Love, in this new life, is no longer a scarce resource. Love, when guarded by grace and nurtured by forgiveness, becomes a safe and generous welcome. It invites genuine connection, where you can be fully known and deeply safe.

Love creates a space where security doesn't cost affection, and affection doesn't threaten security. That is the essence of living.

An Open Road for All Walkers

This path from coping to living is open to all: empaths and narcissists, skeptics and believers, the hurting and the healing. It invites you to take the next step—not with pressure, but with hope.

The journey is personal. But the invitation is for everyone.

As you stand at this threshold—ready to move beyond survival and step into true life—the path ahead beckons with a new invitation: to embrace grace, forgiveness, and Agape love. These are the roots that will nourish your heart and transform the way you love. In the next part of this journey, we'll explore how grace serves as the ultimate boundary that heals, opening doors to deeper connection, freedom, and lasting peace.

Reflection Question

Which qualities—coping or living—do you see most clearly in your life right now? Are you ready to explore grace, forgiveness, and love, and leave coping behind?

Final Thought

Your early choices don't have to write your whole story. Healing grows from a foundation stronger than survival—built on grace that shields, forgiveness that renews, and love that welcomes without condition. This is the narrow path where true life begins, where love and security live not as opposing needs but as a thriving, unified whole.

The journey is yours to take, at your own pace. The invitation stands wide open. Step forward, and watch how new life takes root in places you may have thought were lost.

10

Poetic Reflection of Part 2: Traveling Beyond Survival

Some children learned to hold their breath to keep the peace.
Others learned to smile through tears.
Some became invisible.
Others became fierce.

They did what they had to do.
And it worked—at least for a while.

But even the strongest child deserves more than survival.

Let's keep walking together.

11

Part 3: Transforming the Way We Love

From Fear to Agape Love

"And now these three remain: faith, hope, and love.
But the greatest of these is love."
1 Corinthians 13:13 (NIV)

No matter how fiercely you strive, walking the same rutted trail will only lead you in circles. But what if there's a radically different path—one that fully honors your need for both safety and love? What if it heals the root so the fruit can finally change?

From here forward, we release the old trade-off. No more sacrificing safety for love or love for safety. We embrace both: maximum safety and boundless love. This is a revolutionary breakthrough—a freeing release from the destructive patterns that have held you captive.

Grace swings open the wide door to transformation. Forgiveness invites you inside. And Agape love reshapes everything from within. Grace, forgiveness, and love—Agape flowing through us—shield our hearts while inviting the love, safety, and connection we were always meant to know.

12

Chapter 7: Grace—The Ultimate Healing Boundary

"Because judgment without mercy will be shown to anyone who has not been merciful. Mercy triumphs over judgment."
James 2:13 (NIV)

Together, let's step into this new way of being, starting with Grace. The journey ahead is one of freedom, wholeness, and enduring hope.

When Love Enters the Moment

Grace is Agape love expressed in real time. It offers a transformational shift in how we relate. Often, it begins with connection—affirming, acknowledging, or appreciating the other person. Then, with courage and clarity, it guides the conversation toward healing and unity, away from harm.

Grace disarms pride without silencing truth. It restores dignity rather than asserting dominance. It doesn't merely change the temperature of a room; it softens the entire posture of a heart.

The Meeting: A Fictional Story

David entered the meeting with unshakable confidence, speaking as if he were always right. Across from him, Sarah could barely finish a sentence before being cut off. His tone, posture, and clipped responses sent a clear message: "I know better."

Sarah felt the sting of dismissal. She could have withdrawn or fought to be heard. Instead, she chose a different way. Taking a steady breath, she met his gaze. "David, I see that you're passionate about your ideas, and I respect that. But my perspective has value too. Let's work together instead of proving who's right."

A pause.

Confusion flickered across David's face, then softened into reflection. The tension eased. In that moment, Sarah introduced something stronger than ego—Grace. She reminded them both that every voice matters.

Grace Understood

As David talked over her, Sarah began with a de-escalating compliment (I respect that). That created space for her to speak the truth (My perspective). She followed with a unifying statement (Let's work together). Grace elevated the standard and rebalanced their footing. Here's how it works:

Step 1: Form a connection

Step 2: Speak the truth

Step 3: Offer a unifying direction

Grace doesn't always bring change. But when it doesn't, that may be your clearest signal to step back or walk away. We'll explore those options later in the chapter.

Grace is often defined as unmerited favor or undeserved kindness. That's true, but in relationships it's more than gentle words or restrained emotion; it's strength wrapped in compassion. Grace protects without punishing, speaks truth without aggression, and nurtures connection without surrendering dignity.

As we are reminded: "Let your conversation be always full of grace, seasoned with salt, so that you may know how to answer everyone" (Colossians 4:6, NIV).

This kind of Grace isn't passive. It's intentional. It opens space for connection, truth, and growth.

Grace Through a Psychological Lens

What Sarah modeled reflects more than intuition—it mirrors psychological insight. Grace closely parallels Carl Rogers' concept of unconditional positive regard: accepting others without enabling harm. It creates room for compassion while holding healthy boundaries. Grace allows for failure without forfeiting accountability. It welcomes disappointment without retaliating. It nurtures growth not by lowering standards but by raising understanding. It chooses patience over punishment, softens reactivity, and invites progress.

But here's the difference: most psychological tools help after we've already decided we're worthy of healing. Grace steps in before that decision. It doesn't fix people—it receives them. And in that receiving, transformation begins.

Grace breathes safety into the soul and worth into the moment.

A Difficult Time I Tried: A Personal Story

Understanding Grace in theory is one thing; living it under pressure is another.

I remember a time I tried to set a boundary, but it was anything but graceful. I had spent years absorbing discomfort and avoiding conflict. When I finally spoke up, the words came out rushed, raw, unfiltered. It didn't feel like Grace. It felt like panic.

But then I remembered a verse: "With your feet fitted with the readiness that comes from the gospel of peace" (Ephesians 6:15, NIV). I didn't feel peaceful. But I could still choose peace. I didn't need to be flawless—just willing to try.

That truth steadied me. Grace, I learned, isn't about perfect delivery. It's about readiness. It's the willingness to act in love, even when it feels uncomfortable.

Over time, I've noticed something important: people with narcissistic traits often project Grace well. Calm words, serene tones, the appearance of peace—it's all there. But the sincerity is often missing. Empaths, on the other hand, overflow with sincerity. Their compassion runs deep. But without structure, it can lead to self-neglect. The structure is to "simultaneously" love your neighbor as yourself.

In this way, narcissists and empaths aren't opposites. They're mirrors. One offers structure without heart. The other carries heart without structure. Most of us carry elements of both. Real Grace requires both. Wherever you're starting, the path is the same: practice Grace from the inside out. Let it be sincere. Let it be strong.

What Grace Gives Us

Grace isn't just a virtue—it bears real fruit:

- **Freedom from Resentment:** Grace loosens the grip of bitterness. It cuts the cord to pain that no longer defines you.
- **Stronger Relationships:** Grace fosters trust. When people feel safe being themselves, intimacy deepens.
- **Healthy Boundaries:** Grace says, I value you, and I value myself. It creates clarity where there's confusion.
- **Emotional Maturity:** Grace expands patience, sharpens understanding, and deepens our ability to love well.
- **Spiritual Alignment:** Grace reflects God's heart.

Pause and imagine: what might change if Grace—not fear or frustration—led the way in your relationships?

A Parent-Teacher Meeting: A Fictional Story

Mrs. Carter, a high school teacher, braced for the meeting. An angry email from Mr. Reynolds had accused her of unfair grading. Now he sat across from her, arms crossed, voice tight. "You're not being fair. Jake worked hard."

She could have grown defensive. Instead, she chose Grace. "I can see you care deeply about your son. That's a good thing. Let's look at his work together and see how we can support his growth."

Her response shifted the tone. The confrontation became a conversation. As they reviewed the assignment, clarity replaced blame. What could have become a power struggle turned into a partnership. That's the gift of Grace. It doesn't demand perfection. It simply offers a better way forward.

When Grace Feels Hard

Some relationships make Grace difficult. Sharp words, repeated wounds, or deep tension wear us down. But many harsh behaviors are rooted in unhealed pain. Recognizing this doesn't excuse harm, but it helps us respond without becoming harmful ourselves.

Jesus modeled this perfectly. As He hung on the cross, He prayed: "Father, forgive them, for they do not know what they are doing" (Luke 23:34, NIV). In the face of cruelty, He offered mercy. His Grace didn't erase the pain. He loved them through it.

Psychologically, Grace builds empathy and self-regulation. It teaches us to see beyond behavior to the fear or wounding underneath.

Let's be clear: Grace is not passivity. It's not staying silent when you're harmed. It's not enduring toxicity in the name of love. Grace includes boundaries.

It can sound like this:

"I care about you, but I won't engage in this kind of conversation."

"I'm willing to talk, but not with raised voices."

Grace is honest. It's kind. And it's strong. It's the courage to stay present—

heart open, voice steady—when fear tells you to run or retaliate.

Reflection Question

Here's the practical formula we've discussed:

- **Form a connection**
- **Speak the truth**
- **Offer a unifying direction**

Which of these steps is most difficult for you?

A Final Thought

Grace protects dignity and fosters healing. It turns conflict into collaboration. And because of that, Grace is the ultimate boundary that heals and restores.

But what about the places where connection feels impossible? Grace can transform conversations, soften pride, and protect dignity—but some moments are beyond simple repair. What happens when the ground beneath a relationship has already crumbled? When trust is shattered, when wounds run so deep they echo through years of silence?

Grace doesn't stop at the surface. It doesn't just smooth over tension or calm a room. It walks into the ruins—where love seems lost—and plants seeds where life feels impossible. This is where Grace reveals its truest strength.

When Grace Meets the Ruins

Grace is unmerited favor—unearned kindness that refuses to make flaws the measure of worth. It sounds like Agape love, and it is, but in a very specific form: it meets you in the present. Grace doesn't ignore imperfection; it sees value in the midst of it.

In a world that demands performance before compassion, Grace offers love first.

You feel it when someone listens without rushing to correct. When someone stays present even when your edges are sharp. Grace chooses connection over ego. It doesn't just see who you are—it reaches toward who you're becoming.

Scripture echoes this heart: "For I know the plans I have for you, declares the Lord, plans to prosper you and not to harm you, plans to give you hope and a future" (Jeremiah 29:11, NIV). These words weren't spoken to the triumphant but to the displaced—the discouraged, unsure how to begin again. Grace enters precisely that kind of moment. Not after we've rebuilt. In the ruins.

The Sacred Tension: Love, Truth, and Movement

Grace isn't soft, blind, or pretending everything is fine. Its power lies in holding love and truth together, then moving with both.

Without love, truth cuts too sharply. Without truth, love becomes flimsy and enabling. Grace binds them into something stronger—motion toward restoration.

We see this in the life of Jesus. When religious leaders brought Him a woman caught in adultery, demanding punishment, He shifted the spotlight: "Let any one of you who is without sin be the first to throw a stone at her" (John 8:7, NIV).

No stones fell. No one remained. Then He turned to her:

"Then neither do I condemn you," Jesus declared. "Go now and leave your life of sin" (John 8:11, NIV). This moment reveals the tension Grace holds. Jesus neither condemned nor condoned. He dignified her humanity and pointed her higher. Grace doesn't shame, and it doesn't excuse. It transforms.

What Grace Does That Psychology Can't

Psychology can explain how your brain works. It can build resilience, improve communication, and offer coping tools. But it can't breathe worth into someone. It can't create the fertile safety where transformation begins.

Grace recognizes worth that isn't earned. It says, "You matter right now, even before you get it right."

It creates a space secure enough for truth to land and loving enough for it to be bearable.

Psychology can identify dysfunction and refine coping skills. Grace roots itself in identity and calls forth wholeness.

Grace as a Boundary: The Strongest Invitation

Grace isn't passivity, and it isn't lashing out. "I'll keep absorbing the damage," isn't grace.

A better definition might sound like this: "This is who I am. This is what matters. And I care enough about us to stay kind while staying honest."

In this way, Grace becomes one of the most courageous boundaries you can offer a steady place between chaos and control.

Grace in Motion: A Personal Story

I remember a conversation where I almost retreated into silence. I wanted to shut down or push back on anything to feel safe. But I paused and asked a better question:

What would actually help here?

Not just what would protect me, or settle the score, but what would move this moment forward.

So I said, "Let's not look for who's to blame. Let's figure out how to go forward from here."

The tone shifted. The wall dropped.

Grace had entered, not as a conclusion, but as a beginning. And that was enough.

Grace When It's Least Deserved: A Fictional Story

Jonathan sat alone at the kitchen table, staring at a plate he didn't touch. His wife, Mara, stood at the counter with folded arms, eyes red but dry. This wasn't their first fight. And this time, his words had cut deep.

"I don't know why I always do this," Jonathan muttered, more to himself than to her.

"You always say that," Mara replied, voice brittle. "You say you're sorry, and then it happens again."

Jonathan didn't argue. He didn't defend. For once, he didn't run.

"I'm not asking you to forget," he said quietly. "I'm just asking you to see I'm still trying to be more than the worst parts of me."

Mara turned, softened. "I know you are. But I can't carry it alone."

"I don't want you to."

She took a breath, then sat down across from him. Silent. But she didn't walk away.

That was Grace. Not pretending it didn't hurt. Not rushing toward resolution. Just showing up in the ruins with a willingness to move forward.

Reflection Question

Where in your life—whether in a relationship, a habit, or even your self-talk—could Grace open a new path you wouldn't normally take?

Final Thought

Grace holds truth and love in equal tension, moving both toward action.

It doesn't fix first and love second. It loves first and then transforms.

Best of all, Grace doesn't ask you to start strong. It simply invites you forward.

But Grace isn't just a feeling—it's a practice. And like any practice, it can be strengthened. In the next section, we'll explore how to build relationship skills that keep Grace alive in everyday moments.

Building Relational Skills Through Grace

Tension hangs in the air before it even breaks the surface.

Sarah had just come through a tough day with a new manager. Her words were sharp, tinged with hurt. Instinctively, Sarah could have defended herself or withdrawn.

But instead, she paused. She took a slow breath and answered gently: "I hear how hard this is for you. Let's face this together."

That simple kindness softened the energy in the room. What could have erupted into conflict became a bridge for honest, healing conversation. The tension didn't vanish, but the relationship grew stronger.

This moment holds the heart of Grace—creating space to move away from pain without letting it divide us.

Grace as a Daily Discipline

Grace isn't a rare act reserved for moments of peace. It's a daily choice—a spiritual muscle strengthened by practice.

You won't always get it right. That's okay. Keep working the muscle, and it will grow stronger.

Every disagreement, every misunderstanding, every emotional sting is an invitation. A chance to practice patience, empathy, and courage all at once.

And here's the deeper truth we've explored throughout this journey: love without truth risks enabling harm. Grace walks the narrow path where love, safety, and truth meet.

Guiding Principles for Cultivating Grace

Here are some ways to keep building that path:

- **Choose empathy over judgment.** Before reacting, pause and wonder: What might this person be carrying? Compassion opens the door to loving response without excusing harm.
- **See the bigger story.** When hurt runs deep, it's easy to get stuck in the moment. Grace steps back and asks, What kind of relationship do I want to build? What legacy do I want to leave? Healing—not winning—becomes the goal.
- **Speak with kindness and clarity.** Truth and gentleness are partners. "A gentle answer turns away wrath, but a harsh word stirs up anger" (Proverbs 15:1). Words that combine honesty with care invite openness instead of defensiveness.
- **Set healthy boundaries with love.** Saying no can feel hard, but it protects your well-being while honoring others. Boundaries create the safety that trust needs to grow.
- **Offer feedback with courage and care.** Honest, loving feedback fosters growth. Criticism without Grace only builds walls.
- **Practice patience with others and yourself.** Transformation is a journey. You'll stumble. So will those you love. Every choice to act with Grace plants seeds of maturity and peace.

Grace is strength anchored in conviction yet softened by compassion. It isn't easy. But it's always worth it.

Navigating Difficult Conversations

When conflict comes, having a steady framework helps. Think of it as a triad—Love, Truth, and Action:

- **Lead with love.** Begin by affirming the other person's worth. Even in hurt, remember they are beloved. This softens hearts.
- **Speak the truth.** Grace doesn't sweep problems under the rug. Share honestly how you feel and how actions affect you.
- **Invite a better way forward.** Offer a path that honors integrity and respect.

For example, if someone dominates conversations, you might say: "I appreciate your passion and ideas. How can we make space so everyone's voice is heard?" This names the issue gently, affirms their value, and invites collaboration.

If tension stays high, you could say: "It seems like we're both overwhelmed. Maybe we should pause and revisit this when we're calmer." This doesn't avoid the issue or escalate it. Instead, it protects peace and keeps the door open.

More practical ideas are in Appendices A and B.

"Speaking the truth in love, we will grow to become in every respect the mature body of Him who is the head, that is, Christ" (Ephesians 4:15, NIV). Grace lives at the intersection of truth, security, and love—and from that place, transformation begins.

Signs of Grace-Fueled Growth

Practicing Grace leads to quiet but powerful shifts:

- You respond intentionally, not reactively.
- Conflicts become openings for understanding.
- Peace grows even before every problem is solved.
- Self-awareness sharpens you; you notice triggers and navigate better.
- Empathy expands you; you see others fully, without excusing harm.

Journaling these moments can deepen your insight:

- Where have I grown in kindness or patience?
- What situations still challenge my Grace?
- How am I setting boundaries that honor both me and others?
- What patterns reveal new opportunities or warnings?

Not every relationship will flourish, even with Grace. Sometimes, Grace means stepping back to protect your well-being. But the person you become—rooted in strength, love, and security—is the truest victory.

Reflection Question

Think about a recent difficult conversation. How might responding with Grace have shifted it? What wiser step could you take next time to invite a better path forward?

Final Thoughts

Choosing Grace builds resilience, peace, and connection.

These aren't just words. They are a way of life—one intentional choice at a time.

Grace begins as a single choice, but it grows stronger with practice. Each moment of patience, each step toward honest yet kind connection, lays another stone on the narrow path of love and security working together.

In the next section, we'll explore seven practical paths, specific ways to apply Grace that nurture stronger relationships, deeper peace, and a heart aligned with both truth and love.

The Seven Paths of Grace: Practical Tools

You've seen how Grace reshapes relationships in everyday moments. But what does it look like in practice—step by step?

These seven paths of Grace aren't lofty ideals. They're practical tools you can use daily to respond with strength, dignity, and love—even in the hardest relationships. Grace isn't soft or passive; it's discerning love in motion. Each path shows a different way Grace can show up—not as a fleeting feeling, but as an intentional choice, rooted in both Scripture and sound psychology.

1. The Path of Centered Presence

Tool: Stay in your body before you speak.

Grace begins with presence. Before reacting, pause. Feel your feet on the floor. Notice your breath. When you're centered, you can respond instead of react.

Paul wrote, "Let your gentleness be evident to all. The Lord is near" (Philippians 4:5, NIV). Presence makes gentleness possible. It reminds you that you're not alone—and you don't have to rush.

Psychologist Dan Siegel calls this "name it to tame it." Recognizing your emotions gives them room to settle. Grace isn't performance—it's posture. The first move is inward: grounding before giving.

2. The Path of Connection First

Tool: Begin with a shared value or sincere affirmation.

Whether you're setting a boundary or speaking a hard truth, starting with connection opens hearts. Jesus often began with compassion before correction. Grace forms a bridge first.

Psychologically, this aligns with attachment repair. People hear truth better when they feel safe. A simple phrase can change the tone: "I care about you," or, "We both want what's best here."

3. The Path of Truthful Clarity

Tool: Speak what's true without blaming.

Grace doesn't avoid hard conversations. It delivers truth with courage and honor. Ephesians 4:15 calls us to speak the truth in love—not with blame or passive aggression, but with clarity.

Try this format:

When X happens, I feel Y. I'd like to move toward Z.

Example: When you cancel plans at the last minute, I feel unimportant. I'd like us to plan in ways we can both rely on.

This aligns with nonviolent communication, separating behavior from identity. Grace keeps dignity intact while naming what must change.

Rent Again? A Fictional Story

Jane longed to be a gracious mom. But when her adult son Harry showed up—again—with another crisis and the same excuses, she felt torn. He was late on rent, blaming his boss, needing help.

She listened. Stayed kind. But instead of rescuing, she said: Harry, I love you too much to keep pretending this pattern is okay. I'll help you brainstorm solutions, but I can't fund this one.

Harry stormed off, later texting, "I thought you loved me."

Jane's heart ached—but her peace remained. Grace stayed grounded in truth.

4. The Path of Boundaried Compassion

Tool: Offer support without over-functioning.

Empathy becomes enabling when you take responsibility for someone else's growth. Grace isn't rescuing.

Galatians 6:2 (NIV) says, "Carry each other's burdens," but a few verses later adds, "Each one should carry their own load" (Galatians 6:5, NIV). The distinction matters: we help with what's too heavy, not what each person must learn to lift.

In psychology, this is the line between co-dependence and interdependence. Grace trusts that discomfort can grow people. Love without truth becomes enabling—or even manipulative.

5. The Path of Measured Response

Tool: Slow the moment down.

Urgency shouldn't hijack wisdom. If emotions flood, step back. Say, "I need a moment to think about that," or "Can we revisit this later?"

Even Jesus withdrew to quiet places before major decisions (Luke 5:16, NIV). Clarity rarely comes from reactivity. Pause long enough to reclaim your peace.

6. The Path of Redemptive Curiosity

Tool: Ask a question before offering judgment.

Instead of assuming motive, invite understanding: "Can you help me see what was happening for you?" or "What did you need in that moment?"

Jesus often used questions to disarm shame and invite honesty: "Do you want to get well?" "Why are you afraid?"

Curiosity softens defensiveness and re-engages empathy. Spiritually, it's discernment; psychologically, it's what keeps dialogue open.

7. The Path of Strategic Withdrawal

Tool: Know when to leave well enough alone.

Sometimes, Grace stays. Other times, it steps back. Grace doesn't bind you to toxic patterns—it frees you from them.

Jesus told His disciples, "If anyone will not welcome you, leave that home or town and shake the dust off your feet" (Matthew 10:14, NIV). Leaving isn't failure. Sometimes it's faithfulness—to your calling, your peace, and your safety.

Grace is not consent to mistreatment. It's courage guided by wisdom.

Reflection Question

Which of these seven paths feels most natural to you—and which feels most challenging? How might you stretch into the one you tend to avoid?

Final Thought

Grace protects dignity and fosters healing. It converts conflict into collaboration. It shows you how to show up with presence, love, and truth—especially when it's hard.

But there's one place even Grace can't take you alone: the deeper wounds still holding pain, regret, or injustice. To heal there, you need more than kindness—you need release.

That's where Forgiveness begins.

While Grace opens the door to connection, Forgiveness walks you through it—into the sacred work of letting go, setting free, and reclaiming what harm once stole. It isn't a single act, but a layered process. One that honors your story, protects your boundaries, and restores your dignity without denying what really happened.

As we close this chapter on Grace, prepare to turn the page—to the profound journey of Forgiveness, where love meets healing in the deepest places of the heart.

13

Chapter 8: Letting Go Through Forgiveness

"For if you forgive other people when they sin against you,
your heavenly Father will also forgive you.
But if you do not forgive others their sins,
your Father will not forgive your sins."
Matthew 6:14–15 (NIV)

Forgiveness is love—applied backward in time. It reaches into the past, not to rewrite what happened, but to release the weight you've been carrying. It is retroactive Agape: love that doesn't wait for someone to deserve it, change, or even understand. It chooses peace over punishment. It says, the wound no longer gets to define the future.

Agape love is unconditional, self-giving, and, according to those who believe, rooted in the very heart of God. "While we were still sinners, Christ died for us" (Romans 5:8, NIV). Forgiveness reflects this divine rhythm—it loves even when it hurts, even when it's not returned, even when nothing makes it fair. It is not approval. It is not denial. It is the soul's quiet but fierce declaration: "love is stronger than what was done."

The Freedom You've Been Seeking

Unforgiveness is like a tall glass of poison.
You can set it down, or you can drink deeply,
letting it seep into every part of you.
The choice–and the consequences–are all yours.

Forgiveness doesn't depend on how deeply you feel or how tightly you guard your heart. It doesn't matter if you're rooted in faith, unsure what you believe, or if you think you've already forgiven–or that you never will.

Because at the core, every heart longs for the same things: to feel safe, to be known, to belong. But when those longings mix with unhealed wounds, they can turn into bars. The very things you hold onto for protection–grudges, anger, bitterness–become the walls of your prison.

Forgiveness–often misunderstood, often resisted–is the key that unlocks that door. Not as surrender. Not as weakness. But as a radical act of courage: a decision to stop letting yesterday define today.

Walking Through the Door Grace Opens

Many of us were taught forgiveness was something we do for other people. Maybe you heard, "forgive and forget." Maybe you learned to equate forgiveness with letting someone off the hook, no matter how deeply they hurt you.

But here's the truth worth holding close: forgiveness is first a gift you give yourself.

It is not denial. It's not dismissal. It's not pretending the harm didn't happen. Forgiveness is the choice to lay down the weight of resentment so your heart can breathe again. It's the gift of living freely in the present, no longer chained to the pain of the past.

Some hold on to unforgiveness as a shield–"I'll never forget so this can't happen again." Others cling to anger as justice, convinced forgiveness is weakness. But holding on comes at a cost. It drains your energy. Narrows your vision. Builds barriers that isolate instead of connect. Forgiveness doesn't erase the past–it frees you to decide what the future will hold.

The Hidden Cost of Holding On

Whether your heart opens easily or stays guarded, unforgiveness builds invisible walls.

For empaths, it feels like carrying a backpack of bricks–draining your energy, dimming your joy, and wearing you down day by day. For the self-protective, holding on may feel safer than vulnerability, but the pain festers in silence, robbing you of deeper peace.

No matter your personality or beliefs, unforgiveness is a prison. It keeps old wounds sharp, replaying betrayal on a loop. Forgiveness stops the loop. It doesn't excuse the hurt–it simply refuses to live in it anymore.

A New Lens: The Power of Reframing

So how do you begin to let go?

One powerful step is reframing. Choosing to see the person or moment that hurt you through a wider, more compassionate lens. Reflect on what you've learned about narcissistic and empathic traits. What might have driven their harm? Can you begin to see they were a hurting human being, struggling to survive?

Indeed, they could have–and should have–done better. That's not the point. Forgiveness doesn't say what happened was okay. It simply means you're willing to consider the whole picture–the fears, brokenness, and limitations behind someone's actions. When you see someone as more than their worst moment, forgiveness becomes possible.

Consider Joseph in the Bible. Betrayed by his brothers and sold into slavery, he later told them, "You intended to harm me, but God intended it for good to accomplish what is now being done, the saving of many lives"

(Genesis 50:20, NIV). He didn't deny the pain. He reframed it, and in doing so, he found freedom.

Whether or not you believe in God, reframing loosens the grip the past has on your present. It creates space for healing to take root.

Forgiveness: Strength in Action

The Apostle Paul wrote, "Get rid of all bitterness, rage and anger, be kind and compassionate, forgiving each other, just as in Christ God forgave you" (Ephesians 4:31–32, NIV).

Forgiveness isn't weakness. It's strength—the strength to reclaim your life from bitterness. Even if you don't share that faith, the wisdom still stands: forgiveness is choosing peace over torment, healing over hardness, movement over stagnation.

Walking the Path of Forgiveness

Forgiveness isn't a single moment. It's a practice—as often as needed. You may have to forgive the same person for the same act many times over. The feelings may still come back. Suppressing the anger isn't the same as releasing it.

Start by identifying who or what you're still holding onto. Is it a person? A painful season? A wound you blame yourself for? Then ask: What exactly am I holding against them or myself? What thoughts keep this pain alive?

Next, reframe what you believe about that person or moment. Search for the humanity. See the fears. Look for even fragments of good. Choose understanding over imprisonment. It's not about excusing—it's about choosing to be free.

In my own story, forgiveness didn't come from forcing myself to forget. It came when I could recall even a single moment of kindness in the storm. When I recognized their flaws—and their humanity—something shifted. Space opened for peace.

I shared earlier how trauma as a child took years from my life. The anger

I carried silently shortened my life expectancy by two decades. That's not surprising. Unrelenting bitterness takes a toll on both body and mind. Yet here I am, living past what was expected. I finally put down that wretched glass of poison. And so can you.

Forgiveness gives you the freedom to choose what comes next. You might set boundaries. You might walk away. Or you might rebuild slowly. Forgiveness does not require reconciliation—but it releases you from the burden of bitterness.

Reflection Question

Think of a person you have not forgiven. How does that feel in your body, in your spirit? Would you choose the peace that forgiveness offers?

A Final Thought

Whether you come to this moment from empathy, fear, faith, doubt, or even exhaustion, forgiveness is a doorway. Fill your soul with retroactive agape love. See their humanity—not to excuse, but to understand.

Make a deliberate choice. Step out of your pain and into your peace.

The Seven Tools of Forgiveness

The tools below are practical ways to begin or continue that journey. To help you walk this path, here are seven practical tools rooted in Scripture and psychology that honor your boundaries and your heart:

1. Name the Wound Honestly

Tool: Say the harm clearly without spiritualizing, exaggerating, or sugarcoating it.

Before forgiveness can begin, we have to name what happened. This doesn't mean accusing or endlessly rehearsing the pain. It means speaking the plain truth. Psychology calls this validating your experience. Scripture agrees: "Have nothing to do with the fruitless deeds of darkness, but rather expose them" (Ephesians 5:11, NIV).

Naming the wound lays the foundation for healing. We cannot mend what we refuse to name.

2. Release the Right to Retaliate

Tool: Surrender the desire to get even.

This doesn't mean pretending you weren't hurt. It means refusing to become the kind of person who returns wounds. "Do not take revenge. It is mine to avenge; I will repay," says the Lord (Romans 12:19, NIV).

Psychology shows revenge rarely satisfies; it reactivates injury and prolongs distress. Letting go doesn't mean what they did was okay—it means you refuse to let their harm dictate your next step.

3. Acknowledge the Grief

Tool: Let yourself mourn what was lost.

Forgiveness often follows some kind of loss—a broken relationship, shattered trust, lost time. You may feel let down. Give yourself permission to grieve. Jesus wept at Lazarus's tomb, even knowing resurrection was coming.

4. Allow for Emotional Ambivalence

Tool: Let conflicting emotions coexist without rushing them away.

It's normal to feel anger and compassion, sorrow and peace, clarity and confusion—sometimes all at once when working through forgiveness. The Psalms are full of emotional ambivalence—raw cries for justice mingled with praise and hope.

Psychology calls this emotional integration: the capacity to hold opposing feelings without forcing quick resolution. Forgiveness often comes in waves. Allowing ambivalence gives space to heal honestly and at your own pace.

The Story of Bonny and Phil: A Fictional Narrative

Bonny sat at the kitchen table, staring at her phone. The text from her brother Phil blinked on the screen: "Can we talk?" It had been three months since their last interaction—an argument over unpaid bills that reopened old wounds.

Phil had a pattern: borrow money, make promises, disappear. Their parents always said, "He means well." But Bonny knew good intentions don't pay rent or rebuild trust.

She picked up the phone, then set it down again.

Her husband entered. "You okay?"

"I don't know," she said. "I want to forgive him, but I don't trust him. I love him, but I'm not ready for him in my life right now."

He nodded, knowing better than to rush her.

Looking out the window, she said, "I think I can wish him well... from here. From a distance. That's what I'm ready for."

And that was the truth. She didn't need to explain it—she just needed to live it. That day, she replied with grace and honesty: "I'm not ready to talk yet. But I hope you're finding your way."

Forgiveness doesn't always mean reconciliation. It means choosing peace in how you carry the wound.

5. Choose Not to Be Defined by the Offense

Tool: Don't build your identity around the pain.

Pain may shape you, but it doesn't have to define you. Forgiveness says, "This happened to me, but it is not who I am." Isaiah 61 promises God gives "a crown of beauty instead of ashes." But we must release the ashes to receive the crown.

Psychology calls this post-traumatic growth: emerging stronger and wiser because of—not despite—what you endured. Forgiveness opens the door to that growth.

6. Give It Time and Keep Giving It to God

Tool: Make forgiveness a process, not a performance.

Forgiveness is rarely one-and-done. It's a repeated act of surrender, especially with deep wounds. Jesus told Peter not to forgive seven times, but seventy times seven (Matthew 18:22, NIV). That's not a number—it's a way of life.

In trauma recovery, repetition strengthens healing. Forgiveness may start as a decision, but it matures as discipline. Each time pain resurfaces, you get to choose: bitterness or freedom.

7. Bless Them Without Re-Inviting Harm

Tool: Wish them well without removing wise boundaries.

Instead of remembering someone by an evil act, replace that memory with something positive. This doesn't mean forgetting; it lets you stop reliving their harm. "Joe is a good father and I wish he and his family well," instead of "Joe is the guy who wrecked my car."

Jesus said, "Bless those who curse you, pray for those who mistreat you" (Luke 6:28, NIV). This isn't permission to re-enter dangerous territory. It's a soul-level release. You stop feeding hate and begin watering peace—even if they never change.

Psychology affirms this: those who wish offenders well experience less stress, better immune function, and greater emotional resilience.

Blessing someone doesn't ignore the truth. It affirms their humanity while guarding your dignity.

Reflection Question

Each of these tools is valuable, actionable, and proven to work. How will you implement them in your life? Any person or situation come to mind? How about you?

Final Thought

Forgiveness is remembering differently—without chains. It's not for them. It's for you. It's not about erasing the past; it's about refusing to let it steal your future.

You don't have to feel ready. You just have to be willing.

Alongside these tools, two powerful steps—confession and repentance—open the door to profound healing and freedom. Let's keep walking. Together.

Full Release Through Forgiveness

Two powerful steps release us: acknowledging the truth and choosing change. Often called confession and repentance, these steps hold universal power. Confession means facing the truth about our actions and feelings. Repentance means deciding to take a new path.

Confession and Repentance as Steps Toward Healing

From a psychological perspective, confession is the moment we stop hiding. It's an act of clarity and courage. It's when we say, "Yes, this happened," and allow ourselves to fully see how our choices and experiences have shaped us and affected others. Confession isn't about shame or punishment—it's breaking denial and stepping into clear self-awareness.

Repentance is the next step forward. It's more than remorse. It's the decision to stop repeating what harms. It marks a turning point of honesty and intention. Where confession brings clarity, repentance brings release. Together, they open the door to real growth.

The Bible offers a powerful image of this in Psalm 51. After a devastating personal failure, King David cries out, "Create in me a pure heart, O God, and renew a steadfast spirit within me" (Psalm 51:10, NIV). He's not just asking for forgiveness—he's asking to be changed. That's the heart of repentance: not punishment, but transformation. Psalm 51 is sometimes called the key of David for good reason. While psychology helps us understand patterns, Psalm 51 reaches deeper, inviting us into heart-level renewal that transcends logic.

When understood this way, confession and repentance become freeing, not heavy. They aren't about paying a debt. They're about reclaiming the power to change and grow.

A Moment of Release: A Personal Story

In my healing journey, I believed I had forgiven everyone who had hurt me. Forgiveness came naturally to me as an empath. But then I began praying Psalm 51—not just reading it, but praying it as a personal plea for restoration. I made it part of my emotional housekeeping, asking for clarity and renewal.

One morning, something surprising happened. I woke from a dream with a wave of anger. That emotion felt foreign to me. Sitting with it, I realized the dream had unearthed someone long buried in my mind—someone I had never truly forgiven. I had written them off. I'd stopped seeing them as a person and reduced them to a painful memory. Objectified. In doing so, I had quietly dehumanized them to avoid the ache. I told myself, "they didn't matter, so forgiveness wasn't necessary." But that morning, I knew better. I needed to see them again, as human, flawed, and real. Only then could I begin to let go.

I chose to separate the harm from the person. And then, to complete the release, I prayed for the good in them. I blessed what was still alive in their story. For those who don't pray, sending hope or heartfelt wishes can carry similar grace. That simple act—that choosing—lifted the burden and kept it from returning.

That was a moment of confession and repentance. Not a public declaration, but a quiet shift within. I had to face the truth: I had held onto power in the form of distance. And choosing differently released me.

The Psychological Power of Truth and Change

Confession and repentance are transformative tools—whether directed outward or inward. They help shed shame, dissolve resentment, and propel you forward. When we refuse to face the truth, we stay stuck in cycles of blame, denial, or avoidance. But when we face it honestly and choose better, we reclaim our peace and integrity.

Forgiving others frees us from bitterness. Forgiving ourselves frees us to grow. Without self-forgiveness, we stay chained to who we used to be. Healing isn't a single event—it's a series of quiet revolutions inside you. It happens each time you name what's real and decide what's next.

Action Steps: Acknowledging and Changing Your Behavior

Here are some action steps to help you along the way:

- **Reflect.** Pause and consider: Is there someone you haven't forgiven? Write down their names. Don't rush.
- **Humanize.** For each name, reflect on their full humanity. What's their

story? What good have they done? They are more than their worst moment. So are you. Remember—truth is the heart of forgiveness.

- **Forgive.** Separate the harm from the person. Forgive, whether or not they deserve it. This is Agape love. Receive the peace that follows.
- **Wish Them Well.** Pray for them if you're able. If not, send your best hope for their healing. Wishing someone well gently loosens the grip of resentment. Your heart re-aligns.
- **Repeat.** Take a breath and move to the next name. With each one, your emotional load lightens.
- **Deep Purge.** Pray Psalm 51. Ask God to remove hidden wounds you may not even remember. Let your heart and mind be cleansed for fresh peace.

Reflection Question

Make forgiveness a regular rhythm. Each time you remember someone who hurt you, ask: Am I still carrying this? Am I ready to release? Gulp of caustic poison or no?

Final Thought

Confession and repentance are not burdens to bear—they are doorways to release and renewal. Naming the truth lays down the weight. Choosing change reclaims your future.

As we begin this journey of confession and repentance, forgiveness unfolds—not merely as a choice, but as a way of life. It becomes a transformative process that reshapes us from the inside out.

Let's walk lighter. Together.

Embracing confession and repentance helps us let go of what holds us back and opens our hearts to renewal. But forgiveness is more than a moment or a single step—it's an ongoing way of living. It transforms how we relate to ourselves and others.

In the next section, we'll explore what it truly means to live out transformative forgiveness—discovering how this continuous journey heals relationships, renews hope, and shapes our hearts.

Living Out Transformative Forgiveness

"Forgiveness isn't weakness—it's narrative control.
It's how you stop being the wounded character in
someone else's story and start becoming
the author of your own healing."

Forgiveness is often spoken of as a lofty ideal—noble, yet distant or hard to grasp. But at its core, forgiveness is a transformative force—a gift we give ourselves as much as to others. It lifts us from the exhausting grip of resentment and bitterness and leads us into freedom, peace, and renewed connection. This inward release creates outward liberation.

Scripture invites us to embrace forgiveness as a path to life. Paul urges: "Get rid of all bitterness, rage and anger, brawling and slander, along with every form of malice. Be kind and compassionate to one another, forgiving each other, just as in Christ God forgave you" (Ephesians 4:31–32, NIV).

Here, forgiveness flows from grace received. It's not just a moral act—it's a healing one. It frees us to let go of what binds us and step into restoration.

Not Denial–But Release

Forgiveness doesn't mean excusing harmful behavior or pretending the pain never happened. Transformative forgiveness is not denial. It's the deliberate release of pain so it no longer erodes your peace. Forgiveness doesn't rewrite the past—it reclaims your future. It loosens the grip the past holds over your present and opens the way forward.

This is especially true when the wounds run deep—when you've faced betrayal or abuse. In those cases, forgiveness becomes an act of profound courage: a declaration that your life is no longer defined by what others did. Jesus' words in Matthew 6:14–15 (NIV) echo this deep spiritual reality: "For if you forgive other people when they sin against you, your heavenly Father will also forgive you. But if you do not forgive others their sins, your Father will not forgive your sins."

Forgiveness, then, isn't just about others—it's about your own healing and spiritual freedom.

It also invites a shift in perspective. Instead of seeing others only through the lens of what they've done, forgiveness invites us to see them through the lens of grace and humanity. This doesn't mean minimizing the damage. It means recognizing that every person carries hidden battles, shaped by wounds we may never see.

Colossians 3:12–13 (NIV) reminds us: "Therefore, as God's chosen people, holy and dearly loved, clothe yourselves with compassion, kindness, humility, gentleness and patience. Bear with each other and forgive one another if any of you has a grievance against someone. Forgive as the Lord forgave you."

Forgiveness is the beginning of rebuilding compassion and empathy. It loosens the grip of bitterness and creates space for inner healing. Can you think of someone you've tried to forgive—but still feel tense around?

Forgiveness reframes how you see them. It doesn't excuse the wrong—it changes your posture toward the pain. You begin to see the other not as a villain, but as a human being—flawed and wounded, just like you. That shift reclaims your strength by shifting how you relate to the story you carry.

Forgiveness as Identity Repair

Sometimes what weighs us down isn't just what happened—but how long we've held onto it. As we explored in Chapter 1, long-buried unforgiveness can root itself into protective behaviors—defensiveness, emotional cutoff, superiority, control. Chapter 3 showed how these patterns, once adaptive, can harden into identities that wall us off from love.

Forgiveness disrupts that cycle. It's not just about healing past pain—it's about dismantling the roles we've adopted to survive it. When you forgive, you don't just free others—you unhook yourself from the behaviors that kept the pain alive. In this way, forgiveness becomes a form of identity repair. It retrieves the parts of you lost in the struggle and opens the door to a way of living that no longer passes harm forward.

A Spiritual Shift

Ultimately, forgiveness opens a spiritual door. It invites God's grace to soften your heart and even bless those who caused harm. Romans 12:14 (NIV) offers a radical challenge: "Bless those who persecute you; bless and do not curse."

Though it may feel unnatural, blessing others aligns you with a higher path—a path of peace, freedom, and spiritual maturity. And in blessing them, something quiet and sacred begins to bless you in return.

Forgiveness does not always mean reconciliation. In some cases, strong boundaries are essential for your safety and well-being. Forgiveness is about releasing bitterness and reclaiming peace, even when the relationship remains distant or broken.

Transformative forgiveness changes you. It reshapes how you move through the world and how you connect with others. It deepens your capacity to love and expands your freedom to live unburdened by the past. It is a powerful step toward healing wounds that once felt permanent.

Reflection Question

In what ways might choosing to forgive—whether or not reconciliation follows—open a new path to freedom and peace in your life?

Final Thought

Forgiveness is the doorway to your freedom—an invitation to live untethered from the pain of the past. It doesn't erase the hurt or excuse the harm, but it transforms how those experiences shape your heart and mind.

As you step through that doorway, your heart begins a new chapter—a chapter rooted in greater freedom, deeper wisdom, and a fuller capacity to love.

In the next chapter, we'll explore how to nurture that capacity, building stronger, healthier connections grounded in the transformative power of love.

14

Chapter 9: Growing the Capacity to Love

"Whoever does not love does not know God,
because God is love."
1 John 4:8 (NIV)

Just as forgiveness sets us free from bitterness, love moves us into fullness. Learning to love well isn't instinctive—it's cultivated, like soil turned and tended before it bears fruit. It grows through practice, through the holy friction of discomfort, and through the quiet courage to stretch beyond what feels easy. "And now these three remain: faith, hope, and love. But the greatest of these is love" (1 Corinthians 13:13, NIV).

Where Love Still Needs to Grow

Some of the most loving people I know don't always feel love in the moment; they act on it. They make a conscious choice to love, especially when it's inconvenient, when their emotions fall short, or when love goes unreturned. It's this deliberate choice that holds love's greatest power.

Love feels easy when it's returned. When kindness meets kindness, when appreciation flows freely, when the cost is low, love seems natural. But love dependent on comfort and convenience is conditional. It fades when patience is tested or forgiveness is required.

Our culture often equates love with chemistry, instant compatibility, or emotional highs. These fleeting experiences can't sustain a deep connection. Real love begins when we move past what feels good and step into *what does good.*

Jesus addressed this directly when He said: "If you love only those who love you, what reward is there? Even the tax collectors do that" (Matthew 5:46 NIV). He invites us beyond that easy, surface-level love to something more profound—love that stretches us, shapes us, and transforms us.

Many of us expect love to be effortless. We think that if it requires work, something is wrong. But the kind of love that lasts and transforms isn't a fleeting feeling—it's a courageous, deliberate choice made again and again, especially when feelings falter.

Moving Beyond Surface-Level Love

Both psychology and Scripture teach that deep love is not rooted in shifting emotions but in trust, self-awareness, and resilience. It grows from commitment and the daily discipline to choose kindness over resentment.

Paul's timeless words offer a vivid portrait: "Love is patient, love is kind. It does not envy, it does not boast, it is not proud. It does not dishonor others, it is not self-seeking, it is not easily angered, it keeps no record of wrongs" (1 Corinthians 13:4–5, NIV).

This love is active and intentional. It doesn't wait for the right feelings to appear; it creates them through choice and grace. It is love tempered by wisdom, setting healthy boundaries without shrinking from vulnerability.

Loving fully requires courage: the willingness to risk discomfort, to offer grace even when undeserved, and to love without certainty of reciprocation.

Expanding Love: A Fictional Story

Mara stirred her coffee, watching the steam rise. Across the table, her father scrolled through his phone, avoiding her eyes. Years of silence had built a wall between them. Their conversations were short and strained. Beneath the silence lived an unspoken longing neither of them could name.

Since childhood, Mara had braced herself for his sharp words, his dismissive tone, and the absence of what she craved most: acknowledgment, respect, and love.

For years, she kept her distance, believing love was a transaction. If he wouldn't meet her halfway, why try?

But recently, something shifted inside her. She began to wonder:

What if love isn't a transaction? What if it's a choice I make regardless of his response?

So here she was—breaking years of silence—choosing love without guarantees.

She no longer expected him to change; that hope had faded. Instead, she embraced that loving him wasn't about fixing him—it was about who she was becoming.

She looked up, met his gaze, and said softly, "Dad, thank you for being you and for all you do."

His surprised look met hers, and in the fragile stillness between them, a barrier began to fall. It wasn't closure or perfection, but movement—a new beginning.

Mara smiled, freed from the past. She loved not because it was deserved, but because love transcends deserving. Love is a gift freely given, a choice that sets us free. It frees us from bitterness, from waiting on someone else's change, and from the prison of needing love to be earned or repaid.

This moment was more than a turning point between father and daughter—it was a testament to love's power to grow when we dare to extend beyond comfort, expectation, and return.

Reflection Question

When you consider someone difficult to love, how might your choice to love them—regardless of feelings or expectations—open the way for new growth in your heart?

A Final Thought

Like Mara, we may never get the version of love we hoped for from someone. But in choosing to love anyway, we unlock a freedom that isn't dependent on the other person's response—just our own growth. We can choose to be filled with love.

So, how do we begin loving like this—beyond comfort and into courage? One of the simplest but most powerful ways is through deep listening.

Deep Listening as a Pathway to Agape

If love is something we become, then listening is one of its purest expressions. One of the most tangible ways love deepens is through the simple yet profound act of truly listening.

And Scripture often calls us to have "eyes to see and ears to hear." In other words, the tools for true connection—and true love—are shared with us so we notice more than mere words and attend to hearts, emotions, and unspoken truths. When we see with care and listen with intention, understanding and love converge, letting us respond with the patience, presence, and compassion that Agape requires.

In a world louder and faster than ever, what if the most loving thing you could offer someone was your silence? Not just hearing their words, but truly seeing and receiving the heart behind them? Surrounded by constant distractions and shallow connections, deep, meaningful listening becomes a quiet revolution.

We live in an age of noise—email alerts, social media pings, busy schedules, and the endless pull of screens. It's easy to forget the profound gift of presence. Most of us hear words daily, but how often do we listen with our whole attention? We scroll while people speak. We form replies before someone finishes. Even our conversations can become performances rather than connections. We've been trained to react, not receive—and in the process, love gets lost.

Deep listening is neither passive nor automatic. It's an intentional choice to slow down, quiet the inner chatter, and offer undivided attention. It moves beyond surface exchanges to hold space for another person's full experience—their hopes, fears, joys, and pain.

This kind of listening is a radical act of love.

Why Listening Matters

Proverbs 17:27 (NIV) says, "The one who has knowledge uses words with restraint, and whoever has understanding is even-tempered." True understanding begins with listening well—being slow to speak and quick to hear. This timeless wisdom reminds us: to love well, we must first seek to understand.

Listening with empathy does more than build understanding. It creates trust and safety. When people feel genuinely heard, they know they can reveal their authentic selves without fear of judgment or interruption. In that space, walls lower, wounds soften, and healing takes root.

Whether you see yourself as a natural listener or someone who struggles with it, the invitation is simple yet profound: listen with intention and heart. Offer your presence as a form of love.

When we listen to the heart of another, the noise fades. We notice when they're distraught or resorting to tactics. And from that place of clarity, we can choose to love wisely—sometimes by engaging, sometimes by stepping back.

Listening Beyond Words

Hearing words is automatic. Listening takes effort. It calls not only on our ears but also our eyes, intuition, and emotional awareness.

Research shows that only about 7% of communication comes from words alone. The rest is expressed through tone, facial expressions, and body language. If we rely only on words, we miss the deeper message. That's why listening with our eyes can be even more revealing than listening with our ears.

Our bodies often speak more honestly than our mouths. A downcast gaze, folded arms, or a shift in tone can reveal fear, sadness, or vulnerability we haven't voiced. This is where emotional intelligence comes in—the ability to recognize and respond to unspoken cues in ourselves and others.

When we listen not just with our ears but with our eyes, hearts, and intuition, we begin to hear what someone's soul is whispering beneath the surface. That's where empathy blooms. It's how trust is built—not by reacting to what's said, but by receiving the whole message someone longs to share, even if they don't yet have the words.

Empathy blooms when we listen well. It means stepping into another's world and feeling what they feel without judgment. It builds bridges between friends, families, coworkers, even strangers.

The Cost of Not Being Heard: A Personal Story

I share this because our experiences shape both how we listen and how deeply we long to be heard.

As a child, I was often overlooked. My parents divided their attention along gender lines, and my father was frequently absent. I shared earlier in Chapter 2 about asking for a slice of pumpkin pie—about my pleas for help with danger that went ignored. I felt invisible, unvalued, and unheard.

That early neglect taught me two things. First, I know how deeply it hurts not to be seen. Full Stop. It hurts. Second, I discovered the quiet power of offering someone else the attention I longed for. I learned to listen with care—a skill born from longing.

Many carry similar invisible wounds, though their stories differ. Interrupting, talking over someone, or glazing over emotionally charged moments aren't small missteps. They fracture connection and reinforce a hidden fear: I'm not worth listening to.

Poor listening doesn't just frustrate communication—it teaches people they don't matter. Over time, it silences voices that ache to be known. Whether or not you recognize this pain in yourself, the need to be truly heard is universal.

In my work with diverse people, I've seen deep listening change lives. Longstanding struggles soften when someone finally listens without rushing to fix or judge. People who were once guarded begin to open. Tears fall. Relief comes. Healing begins—not because advice was given, but because their humanity was seen.

Listening is a healing art.

Listening with Our Whole Being

Listening isn't just a mental exercise—it's an embodied act of love. When we're talking, we're not learning. But when we listen, we receive. We grow. We love more fully.

I listen as much with my eyes as with my ears, probably more so. Body language, facial expressions, subtle shifts in tone—these often reveal more than words can. Nonverbal communication is usually more honest, less guarded. I often will verbally respond to the body language and not the words.

I recall working with a client whose voice sounded steady, but her slumped shoulders and weary eyes told a deeper story. By tuning in to those cues, I could meet her pain where it was most real, even when words failed.

Jesus modeled this kind of listening. In Mark 8:23–25 (NIV), when He healed the blind man, Jesus didn't just speak; He touched the man's eyes and engaged him personally, meeting his need with both care and power. This sacred attention—listening with presence and action—is love in its purest form.

Matthew 13:16 (NIV) says, "But blessed are your eyes because they see, and your ears because they hear." This blessing points to a holy awareness—seeing and hearing beyond the obvious, to the heart.

Patience: The Heartbeat of Love

Deep listening requires patience. It resists the urge to interrupt, rescue, or solve too soon. It embraces the messy, imperfect reality of human emotion.

Patience is the heartbeat of love. 1 Corinthians 13:4 (NIV) reminds us, "Love is patient, love is kind." To love truly is to sit in silence, confusion, or pain without rushing to fix it. It means offering presence and acceptance, allowing healing to unfold in its own time.

This patience extends inward, too. Sometimes it's hardest to listen deeply to our own feelings and needs. Practicing patience inwardly is part of the journey toward Agape love—an unconditional embrace of both others and ourselves.

When we practice deep listening—whether with friends, family, coworkers, or strangers—we create a ripple of healing. One person feels seen and valued. That person then has space to become more authentic, more whole.

Deep listening creates subtle but powerful shifts—often in the quietest moments, when no one is trying to win or defend. Sometimes it begins like this:

Another ripple started one evening, a father and his teenage daughter sat in silence after years of tension. He didn't defend himself. She didn't accuse. Instead, he simply listened as she spoke, really listening for the first time. In that quiet exchange, nothing about the past changed—but the heaviness between them began to lift. It wasn't closure, but it was a beginning.

Reflection Question

How observant are you when someone else is speaking? What do you notice? Do you seek to understand their perspective by attuning your feelings—not to lose yourself, as empaths sometimes do, but to truly connect and allow a deeper, even spiritual, bond to form?

A Final Thought

Deep listening is more than a skill—it's a sacred practice, a powerful form of love. When we listen with eyes, ears, and heart, we offer a gift beyond words: our presence.

When I think back to that slice-of-pumpkin-pie moment, I realize I wasn't craving help—I was craving dignity. That's what deep listening offers: dignity.

This is the love that heals wounds, mends broken relationships, and nurtures peace in the heart.

So, love deeply.
Love wisely.
Love courageously
beyond what feels easy.

Because love is not just something we feel. It's something we become.

The Transformative Power of Agape in Relationships

Have you ever felt the crushing weight of love that's always on trial, where your worth is constantly measured, and you never know if you're enough? It's exhausting, isn't it? The strain of performing, of tiptoeing around someone else's expectations just to hold on to their affection.

Now imagine a love that doesn't keep score. A love that doesn't need proof. A love given freely, without condition. What if the key to healing your relationships isn't found in striving harder, but in surrendering to the most radical love of all: Agape love?

Agape Love: A Different Kind of Foundation

Agape love is like nothing else. It doesn't demand, calculate, or withhold. It sacrifices without expectation. It meets you at your worst, doesn't wait for you to get it right, and never walks away. It doesn't require perfection—it creates space for growth, no matter where you are on your journey.

Conditional love breeds anxiety and the fear of never being enough. It turns affection into a transaction. But Agape love breaks that cycle, freeing us from striving to earn what should be freely given. It liberates us from the need to perform, quiets the fear of rejection, and invites us to rest in love that simply is. That kind of love heals. That kind of love transforms.

What the Heart Needs: The Psychology of Safe Love

From a psychological standpoint, conditional love breeds insecurity. When acceptance is earned, we're always hustling for worth, chasing validation that never lasts. Stress. Anxiety. But Agape love offers emotional safety. It whispers, "You are enough as you are," making space for healing and growth. In this kind of love, we're valued not for what we do, but for who we are. Peace. Healing. Safety.

Seeing Through the Lens of Possibility

Agape love invites transformation. It begins when we stop seeing each other through the lens of flaws and start seeing each other through the lens of possibility. It doesn't try to fix someone into meeting our needs—it gives them the freedom to be human: real, messy, and still worthy of love. That freedom changes everything.

And this kind of love doesn't come from us alone. It flows from the heart of Christ Himself. Jesus loved us not because we deserved it, but because of who He is. Agape love is unearned, unshakable, and willing to bear the cost of our healing.

Grace, Forgiveness, and Love as Transformational Boundaries

Agape love also calls us to live out grace and forgiveness in our relationships. Grace, forgiveness, and love form the foundational boundary that enables true healing and transformation in relationships. These become the gentle strength that protects our hearts and allows connection, even in the face of pain.

One piece of wisdom stands firm: "Bear with each other and forgive one another if any of you has a grievance against someone. Forgive as the Lord forgave you" (Colossians 3:13, NIV).

Grace and forgiveness loosen the grip of resentment. They unbind us from the weight of what went wrong and lead us toward understanding, toward restoration. They create breathing room for relationships to grow and heal. But grace and forgiveness are not an invitation to endure harm without limits. They create space for healing while also giving us clarity to protect what is sacred in ourselves and others.

Another powerful truth offers a deeper layer: "Above all, love each other deeply, because love covers over a multitude of sins" (1 Peter 4:8, NIV). Deep love doesn't pretend everything is fine or ignore what's wrong—it chooses healing over punishment. It protects, mends, and offers grace exactly where it's most needed.

Grace tells us we no longer need to demand justice, because we've already been shown mercy. It's like a soft gate—firm enough to guard what's good, gentle enough to let love in. Forgiveness unlocks the cell of bitterness. Together, these boundaries change the atmosphere of our relationships. They unhook us from the past and open a way forward for others and ourselves.

Start Small: How to Practice Agape Love in Daily Life

If you're unsure where to start, try this: choose one relationship where you've been holding back love out of fear or hurt. Ask yourself, "What would Agape love do here?" You don't have to fix everything today. Just start by offering presence instead of pressure. That's how healing begins.

To receive Agape, you are best advised to give it. Giving is the one piece you do control.

And if it still feels hard to believe or receive, that's okay. Healing doesn't happen all at once. Sometimes the bravest thing you can do is simply admit there's another way. A way that doesn't require perfection. A way that doesn't make you earn love. Agape love meets you where you are—and walks with you, one small step at a time.

Agape love may sound big and abstract, but it often shows up in small shifts—simple choices that gradually change the atmosphere of a relationship. Like this:

When Love Begins to Breathe: A Fictional Story

Weeks had passed since Lena quietly decided to change the way she loved. At first, it was subtle. But slowly, the shift became undeniable. The pressure that had lingered in their relationship began to dissolve. Conversations felt lighter; their time together was more at ease.

One evening, as they sat on the couch, Lena noticed something new. Jake was talking about his day with a kind of freedom she hadn't seen in a long time. In the past, even the smallest exchanges carried an edge, like he was bracing for something to go wrong. But tonight, there was calm.

He paused, his voice gentler than usual. "I know I'm not perfect, Lena. But I don't feel like I'm walking on eggshells with you anymore."

Her heart swelled. This was the change she had hoped for. She wasn't expecting him to be flawless. She wasn't trying to fix him. She was simply there with him, not over him.

She remembered the night she almost corrected him over something small. Fear had welled up—the fear that if she didn't intervene, something would break. But she had paused, taken a breath, and let it go. That night, something shifted—not in him, but in her. That's when the tension began to fade.

"I feel that too," she said, her voice steady and warm. "I'm not waiting for you to be perfect, Jake. I'm here. Just as you are."

Jake's face softened. "I think that's what's been missing. That fear of messing up. It's been weighing on me. But now, I feel like I can just be."

Lena smiled, sensing the quiet ease between them. This wasn't just love—it was freedom. The freedom to be themselves without constantly measuring up.

Agape love, Lena whispered, more to herself than to him.

Jake nodded, his voice low but sure. "I feel like I can finally breathe. Not because I've gotten it all right. But because I know I don't have to."

She reached for his hand. The tension that once defined their relationship had lifted. No walls. No bracing for failure. What had once felt fragile now felt solid—built not on performance, but on grace, patience, and acceptance.

Reflection Question

How might embracing Agape love—with its call to grace and forgiveness—transform how you view and engage in your most challenging relationships?

Final Thought

Agape love doesn't just change us—it changes how we love. When grace and forgiveness become the boundaries we live by, we create space for healing, freedom, and growth. This love doesn't wait for others to be perfect. It offers room to grow, to stumble, to begin again. And in that space, relationships become something new—not only safe, but sacred. When we love with Agape, we don't just reflect Christ's love—we embody it. And in doing so, we become vessels of transformation in our homes, our hearts, and the lives we touch.

If this kind of love feels impossible, you're not alone. None of us arrives there overnight. But there are small, intentional steps you can take to grow your capacity for Agape love. Let's explore seven practical paths that will help you live this out day by day.

The Seven Paths of Agape

We all want to love well. But true, deep, unconditional love—Agape—isn't something that just appears fully formed. It's a choice. A way of living that seeks the good of others, even when it costs us something. It's the kind of love that stays when feelings fade, when mistakes happen, or when trust feels fragile.

Scripture reveals this love as God's heart for us. Psychology helps us understand how to grow it in real life. But the world around us often teaches a very different pattern—what I call transactional love or counterfeit love. That's the love that says, "If you meet my needs, I'll stay. If not, I'll walk away." It's conditional, fragile, and leaves us empty.

Agape love heals what transactional love breaks. It is patient and kind, honest and strong. And here's the good news: it's not beyond your reach. You can grow this kind of love, step by intentional step.

You don't have to master all of these at once. Think of them as invitations—gentle ways to build love's strength, one small choice at a time. Here are the seven paths to help you grow your capacity to love like Christ. Each draws from both Scripture and psychology to guide you forward with grace.

1. Stay Rooted in Source, Not Shortage

Tool: Anchor yourself in Agape love before you try to love others.

You can't pour from an empty cup. Agape begins with being filled, knowing deep in your soul that you are already loved and safe. Psychology calls this secure attachment. It's the foundation that allows you to love without fear of running out.

Scripture reminds us: "We love because He first loved us" (1 John 4:19, NIV). Receiving this love allows it to flow naturally to others.

This is one of the foundational disruptions of true love—learning it from the right source instead of from past wounds or scarcity.

2. Let Compassion Be Stronger Than Judgment

Tool: Choose curiosity over criticism when others fall short.

When someone hurts you, it's easy to close off or lash out. But Agape love invites a deeper question: "What pain might this person be carrying?" In psychological terms, this is perspective-taking—seeing beyond someone's moment of failure to their whole story.

This doesn't mean excusing harm. It simply means refusing to let judgment harden your heart.

Jesus modeled this when He prayed, "Father, forgive them, for they do not know what they are doing" (Luke 23:34, NIV). Compassion keeps love alive, even when circumstances tempt us toward bitterness.

3. Set Boundaries That Protect Love, Not Punish People

Tool: Set limits that guard your energy and keep love sustainable.

Boundaries aren't walls to shut people out; they're fences that protect what is healthy. Without them, love becomes strained or resentful.

Scripture says, "Above all else, guard your heart, for everything you do flows from it" (Proverbs 4:23, NIV). Healthy boundaries guard our capacity to love—they preserve connection instead of depleting it.

This balance is part of the Narrow Path System: protecting love so it can endure.

4. Forgive Frequently—Even in Micro Ways

Tool: Let go of minor offenses quickly to keep love flowing.

Forgiveness isn't reserved for life's biggest betrayals. It's needed in small daily moments—the sharp tone, the overlooked message, the misunderstanding that lingers. Psychology calls this rupture and repair—the small cycles of hurt and healing that keep relationships alive.

Paul reminds us, "Love keeps no record of wrongs" (1 Corinthians 13:5, NIV). You don't have to forget what happened, but you can choose not to carry it like a weight.

Here's how it looks in real life:

The Story of Kevin and Tracy

Kevin sat on the couch, the sting of their argument replaying like a scratchy record in his mind. Tracy had snapped at him again, hurriedly brushing past his offer to help. He knew her stress was heavy, but it still hurt.

Later, she padded into the room. "I'm sorry," she said softly.

Kevin felt the familiar temptation to hold onto the grudge. But then he saw the exhaustion in her eyes.

"I get it," he said gently. "You're carrying a lot. But I need tenderness too. Let's try again."

She nodded, relief washing over her.

Love didn't fix everything that day. But it made room for grace. Agape lives in these small, brave choices—choosing each other again, even on hard days.

5. Hold the Tension of Truth and Grace

Tool: Speak the truth gently, even when it's hard.

Love doesn't mean avoiding hard truths. It means speaking to them in a way that heals instead of wounds. Psychology calls this nonviolent communication—honesty wrapped in kindness.

Paul wrote, "Speaking the truth in love, we will grow" (Ephesians 4:15, NIV). Truth without grace becomes harsh. Grace without truth becomes hollow. Together, they transform.

6. Stay Present in Discomfort

Tool: Remain present when emotions get hard.

Love shows up by staying. It doesn't run from grief, anger, or fear. Psychologists call this emotional attunement—sitting with someone's pain without trying to fix or flee.

Jesus modeled this time and again. He wept with His friends, comforted the outcast, and stayed near suffering people. Love doesn't turn away—it leans in.

7. Choose Daily: Love Is a Practice, Not a Feeling

Tool: Act in love even when emotions lag behind.

Some days, love feels effortless. Other days, it's a deliberate choice you make again and again—pausing before snapping, listening longer than you want to, offering kindness when it would be easier to withdraw.

Psychology calls this behavioral activation—living out your values even before your feelings catch up.

Scripture says, "Put on love, which binds everything together in perfect unity" (Colossians 3:14, NIV). Love is something you wear—a daily practice that shapes your heart over time.

Reflection Question

These seven paths are not steps to perfection—they are invitations to live with more grace, courage, and presence. Which one speaks most deeply to your current season of life?

Final Thought

As you journey along these seven paths of Agape, you're not only growing your capacity to love like Christ—you're cultivating a foundation that shapes every relationship and every choice. Love is both the soil and the seed; it nurtures growth but also calls for wisdom to tend it well.

That wisdom—discernment—is the companion that helps you recognize when to give more love, when to set healthy boundaries, and when to protect your heart and the hearts of those you care about. Discernment keeps love rooted in truth and grace, guiding your steps in complex relationships and decisions.

In the next chapter, we'll explore what discernment really means and how you can train your inner compass to see clearly. You'll meet Heather and Mike, whose story will illuminate how discernment works in real life—helping you navigate relationships with confidence and spiritual authority.

With love as your foundation and discernment as your guide, you're poised to become a healing presence in the world—one relationship, one step at a time.

15

Poetic Reflection of Part 3: Living the Questions

Sometimes healing begins,
not with answers,
but with living the questions.

If you could speak to the child who once chose survival,
who sacrificed love for security,
or security for love
what would you tell them now?

Would you promise they are safe?
Would you tell them they are loved?
Would you show them the way?

And once they understood,
would you encourage them to keep walking?

Let's keep walking together.

16

Part 4: Becoming a Healing Presence in the World

Discernment, Influence and Spiritual Authority

*"Once we have calmed our internal storms,
we can begin engaging the external world
with clarity and courage."*

As we step beyond Part III, pause. Not only to reflect on what love means to you, but to notice how psychology and Scripture breathe life into your journey right now. Could it be that psychology, a field rooted in inquiry, is uncovering truths already woven into the fabric of Creation—whispers of Divine design? And how might the timeless words of Scripture meet you—sometimes boldly, sometimes like a breath you didn't know you were holding—speaking directly into your deepest longings?

Over the years, I've watched these two streams—modern science and ancient revelation—intertwine in ways that feel less like coincidence and more like choreography. Perhaps you've sensed it too: quiet echoes, repeated truths, a shared melody of who we are and what we ache for. You don't have to agree—only stay curious. Listen with an unclenched heart. Explore the edges of what you thought you knew, then lean beyond them.

Though born in different centuries and shaped by different methods, these sources converge to reveal the same hidden terrain of reality. Sometimes we welcome their messages eagerly; other times, doubt or resistance rises like morning fog, blurring what once felt clear. Yet beneath it all, we travel the same path—each at our own pace, each carrying the weight of our own questions.

Wherever you stand—seeking growth or living in freedom, wrestling with old wounds or basking in new light—your experience is valid and unrepeatable. This isn't a contest of right and wrong but an invitation into honest self-awareness that heals.

So hold this space with gentle curiosity. Ask bold questions. Lean into the discomfort. Draw nearer to what is real. Each step draws you closer to love that heals rather than harms, connection that frees rather than confines, and faith that lifts rather than limits.

Part III helped you still the storm within and find love's unshakable ground. Now Part IV asks: What happens when that inner calm begins to ripple outward and change the world beyond yourself?

Perhaps you've already felt it—the childhood fears loosening their grip like fading shadows, the quiet courage rising to face hidden pain, the grace of forgiveness soaking into wounded places like soft rain falling on thirsty soil. This transformation isn't a surface change; it is a rebirth of spirit and mind. As your capacity for agape love expands, so does your freedom to think clearly, respond intentionally, and recognize when old wounds call not for defense, but for gentle healing.

This is your moment to rise into your truest self. Fear was never your real companion. Love always was. You were carved from the image of a God who is love, not fear—formed to live fully in grace, forgiveness, and love without end.

So, as we begin Part IV, ask yourself: How might I become a healing presence in the world around me? How can the way I live, listen, speak, forgive, and love bring restoration—starting here, starting now?

You don't need every answer. You only need to take the next faithful step.

And what lies beyond the toxic dance? Scripture offers a glimpse: "The kingdom of heaven is like a king who prepared a wedding banquet for his son" (Matthew 22:2, NIV). A banquet—a gathering, a celebration where love flows without fear, without condition, without end.

You were made for that feast. And every step you take toward healing draws you nearer to that radiant table—where joy is not rationed, and love never runs dry.

17

Chapter 10: Building Relational Discernment

A simple act of kindness can reveal more than you expect. Once, I bought a friend a hamburger—just because. The next night, they returned the favor. Same restaurant. Same meal. But something felt off. There was a shift in the air, subtle but unmistakable, like a faint dissonance in an otherwise familiar song. And in that moment, I knew it was time to step back.

What happened? How did something that seemed generous turn into a quiet warning sign?

Transaction.

What True Discernment is

Discernment is more than instinct or intellect; it's the ability to see beneath the surface, separating what is truly good from what only wears the mask of good. Intuition may whisper as a fleeting impression, but discernment tests those impressions against the steady light of wisdom.

At its heart, discernment is an act of love. It listens deeply—not just to words, but to the spaces between them. True discernment slows down enough to see and hear people as they are—not idealizing or dismissing them, but honoring the truth of their story. This deep, compassionate clarity mirrors how Jesus engaged others, noticing what was hidden and responding with both tenderness and truth.

Proverbs 2:6 (NIV) tells us, "For the Lord gives wisdom; from his mouth come knowledge and understanding." Discernment is not merely intellectual—it is spiritual. It grows as we align our hearts with truth larger than ourselves.

Scripture ties discernment to wisdom like a root to a tree. Proverbs 3:21 (NIV) urges, "My son, do not let wisdom and understanding out of your sight; preserve sound judgment and discretion."

Discernment anchors us in what is real, shielding us from being swept away by appearances or emotions. Ephesians 5:10 (NIV) adds, "Find out what pleases the Lord," reminding us that discernment is a living, ongoing pursuit of what is good.

Unlike paranoia or skepticism, discernment doesn't harden into fear or cynicism. Paranoia sees threats everywhere. Skepticism, though sometimes useful, can erode trust until nothing feels safe.

Discernment is different. It clarifies. It teaches us to see motives without malice, to recognize when something is misaligned with truth, and to quietly step away from manipulation cycles into emotional security.

A common misconception is that discernment is just a polite word for being judgmental. But judgment labels others to feel superior. Discernment seeks truth to bring freedom. Judgment closes hearts; discernment opens eyes and restores healthy, safe connections.

The Psychology of Discernment

Even with sharpened awareness, our minds can cloud clarity. We rely on mental shortcuts—heuristics—to make quick decisions. Though often helpful, they can mislead us, especially when emotions or past pain distort perspective. Cognitive biases can disguise flattery as sincerity or control as love. Discernment slices through these illusions and reveals what is real.

One of its greatest gifts is breaking unhealthy relational patterns. Many people unknowingly repeat the same toxic dynamics because they miss the early signs—dismissed concerns, mixed messages, misplaced guilt.

Discernment helps us notice subtle red flags, sometimes even before harm unfolds. And even if we miss the first signals, it's never too late. Every moment of awareness is a step toward freedom.

Psychology helps us understand how the mind works and offers valuable tools for healing, but it often stops at managing thoughts and behaviors. Scripture goes deeper—it doesn't just call us to manage life, but to be transformed by truth that endures beyond us.

Psychology touches pieces of discernment—emotional intelligence, decision-making, bias—but often in fragments. Scripture weaves them into a whole, calling us to live fully in alignment with what is real. Many of our deepest struggles come from clinging to untrue ideas about ourselves and others. The Bible invites us to release those lies and step into a freedom that cannot be taken away.

Hebrews 5:14 (NIV) contrasts maturity with emotional reactivity: "But solid food is for the mature, who by constant use have trained themselves to distinguish good from evil." Discernment isn't innate; it is cultivated through practice, reflection, and a relentless pursuit of truth. As John 8:32 (NIV) reminds us, "Then you will know the truth, and the truth will set you free." The clearer our grasp of truth, the sharper our discernment becomes.

One simple way to train discernment is to pause and ask: "Is this reaction rising from truth—or from emotion?" The more we practice that pause, the more clarity grows.

Sarah and Emily: A Fictional Story

Sarah and Emily had been friends for years. Sarah admired Emily's charisma—how she could light up a room with her presence. But over time, Sarah began to feel a quiet unease, like a faint crack in an otherwise polished surface. Conversations always seemed to pivot back to Emily's needs. When Sarah shared her own struggles, Emily listened—but only briefly—before steering the topic elsewhere.

Then came the subtle betrayals. A personal story Sarah had entrusted in confidence surfaced casually in a group conversation. A decision Sarah made for herself was met not with encouragement but with criticism wrapped as concern. A pattern emerged: Emily's kindness carried unspoken conditions. Admiration, loyalty, and compliance were quietly expected in return.

The turning point came when Sarah hesitated before sharing good news. Instead of joy, she felt anxiety—how would Emily react? That hesitation was the signal she had been missing. Real friendship should never require walking on eggshells or dimming your light to keep someone else comfortable.

Discernment helped Sarah finally see what she had overlooked: Emily's charm was a costume, not a commitment. And in that realization, Sarah felt a surprising calm. She didn't need a dramatic confrontation. She simply stopped over-explaining, stopped justifying, and stopped letting guilt steer her choices.

As she stepped back, the truth grew clear—authentic friendship doesn't demand; it gives freely.

Reflection Question

Can you recall a moment when something that looked or felt good later revealed itself as misaligned with truth? What helped you see it clearly? And what might help you see it sooner next time?

Final Thought

Discernment peels back layers and reveals what is real. It helps us live from integrity and wisdom rather than fear or confusion. Whether navigating relationships, decisions, or your own emotions, discernment offers a quiet compass that never rushes but always points true.

The ability to discern grows stronger with use. Let each step bring you closer to truth—and to the freedom that follows.

With a clearer sense of how discernment shows up in our relationships, the next step is to learn how to actively sharpen this inner compass—so you can respond with wisdom and clarity in the moments that matter most.

Training Your Inner Compass to See Clearly

She felt it a quiet unease, like a shadow flickering at the edge of her awareness. The smile was warm. Yet something didn't align.

And then, one day, the mask slipped. The charm fractured. Truth arrived like a wave crashing into fragile glass, leaving only one haunting question: How did I not see this sooner?

Discernment isn't inherited; it's forged. Each choice, each lesson, each painful revelation shapes the inner compass God uses to help us separate what is genuine from what is false. Without it, we drift—easily swayed by emotion, flattered by charm, caught in patterns we later regret. But with it, clarity emerges like dawn breaking through thick fog. Confidence grows. Wisdom takes root, anchoring us in what is real even when everything else feels uncertain.

Hebrews 5:14 (NIV) reminds us that maturity means learning to distinguish good from evil. Like strength, discernment develops through steady, intentional practice. It refines our ability to recognize what is true, unmask what is hidden, and respond wisely rather than react impulsively.

Building Discernment: A Personal Story

When I first began training my inner compass, I learned a humbling truth: kindness doesn't always equal sincerity. Some people, though warm on the surface, conceal motives very different from their words—what Scripture calls wolves in sheep's clothing.

I hadn't planned to study selfishness, but discernment kept leading me there. Time after time, I saw how charm could disguise control, and how kindness could become a subtle weapon. These realizations—and the patterns they revealed—became the foundation for Appendices A & B. They are not just information; they are a map to help you see these dynamics far sooner than I once did.

Then I uncovered another layer: narcissism. At its core, it is selfishness turned inward—like the myth of Narcissus, so captivated by his own reflection that he could no longer see anything else. Narcissism is often less malice than it is pain—a survival strategy stretched beyond its limits until it collapses into self-absorption.

What surprised me most was how easily I overlooked the signs—not because they weren't there, but because I had been trained to explain them away. From childhood, many of us are taught to just be nice, not to judge, or give the benefit of the doubt, even when something inside whispers otherwise. That cultural conditioning dulls discernment, leaving us vulnerable to manipulation we should have seen coming.

Studying these traits was invaluable. It helped me see narcissism for what it is, recognize the early signs, and have compassion. To support you in building that same clarity, I've outlined common patterns—and their biblical counterpoints—in the appendices. Naming what's hidden is the first step toward seeing what's true.

The design of this book intentionally meets you where you are, guiding you to grow in both empathy—the gateway to Agape love—and discernment, the guardrail that protects it. Step by step, layer by layer, you've been shedding what no longer serves you. What once felt like a necessary mask is giving way to quiet strength, deeper grace, and a truer, more grounded version of yourself.

The Role of Practice in Discernment

Every day offers small, ordinary chances to sharpen discernment. How we respond to challenges, assess relationships, and interpret situations either strengthens or dulls our inner compass. Some suggestions:

- **Pause Before Reacting.** Emotional reactions often cloud judgment. A breath creates space for wisdom to rise. Proverbs 14:29 (NIV) says, "Whoever is patient has great understanding, but one who is quick-tempered displays folly." Pausing helps you see beyond impulse.
- **Test Your Thoughts and Emotions.** Feelings are real, but they aren't always right. Cognitive biases—like confirmation bias, which favors what we already believe—can twist perception. Philippians 4:8 (NIV) urges us to "dwell on whatever is true, noble, right, pure, lovely, and admirable—if anything is excellent or praiseworthy, think about such things." In practice, this means filtering emotions through wisdom.
- **Seek Counsel from the Wise.** Proverbs 11:14 (NIV) reminds us, "For lack of guidance a nation falls, but victory is won through many advisers." Spiritually and emotionally mature voices help reveal what your own blind spots may miss.
- **Examine Your Biases and Triggers.** Past experiences shape how we see the present. If love was conditional growing up, manipulation can feel familiar. If betrayal left deep wounds, you may over-correct, seeing deceit everywhere. Recognizing these patterns restores balance.
- **Study Behaviors and Patterns.** Manipulation, conditional love, and selfishness rarely appear random. They follow predictable scripts. This book—and the appendices—help you name those scripts in yourself and others, strengthening discernment like a muscle.

Tria and the Hidden Motive: A Fictional Story

Tria sat across from her coworker, who pitched a new project with infectious energy—bright ideas, promises of shared success.

But beneath the enthusiasm, she felt it again. A subtle tension. A hunger—not for collaboration, but for control.

She didn't confront him. She didn't accuse. Instead, she asked one quiet question: "Who will this benefit most?"

The pause spoke louder than his answer. His response circled back, not to shared growth, but to personal gain.

No confrontation was needed. Discernment gave Tria clarity—and the freedom to choose wisely. She supported the project but kept a guarded distance from his hidden agenda.

Reflection Question

When uncertainty rises, which practice would help you most—pausing before reacting, testing your thoughts, seeking wise counsel, or watching patterns? How might focusing on just one strengthen your inner compass and guard your peace?

Final Thought

Discernment quietly separates walking blindly into deception from stepping forward with wisdom. It gives you the courage to live with clarity, confidence, and peace—no longer captive to manipulation or misplaced trust.

Every lesson here sharpens your inner compass. Step by step, you train your heart to see what is real, even when the world tries to convince you otherwise. And with each new layer of truth revealed, you'll find yourself living with less fear, more freedom, and a deeper grace that cannot be shaken.

With a clearer sense of how discernment grows within you, our next step will explore how it applies between you and others—shaping the way you engage relationships and make decisions that protect what matters most.

Discernment in Relationships and Decision Making

Anna sat quietly in the café, her gaze steady as he spoke. His words flowed with practiced ease—a melody of charm layered with just enough warmth to feel safe. At first glance, he seemed genuinely captivated by everything she shared.

Yet beneath the surface, something hummed off-key. The way he leaned in just a little too close. The intensity behind his gaze—too sharp, too rehearsed. A whisper rose within her, soft but insistent: Pay attention.

She had walked this path before—with those who knew exactly what to say and precisely when to say it. She had ignored that whisper before, only to find herself entangled in someone else's hidden agenda. But this time, she paused.

As the conversation unfolded, the subtle threads of manipulation revealed themselves—woven into his compliments, buried in his probing questions. A hidden trace of control lingered beneath every word. And suddenly, the fog lifted. It clicked.

Her instincts, once dismissed as overreaction, were discernment's voice—tender yet resolute—guarding her from a truth not yet fully visible.

A soft wave of relief washed over her, like the first breath after surfacing from deep water. For the first time that day, Anna felt the quiet strength of wisdom—not merely as a shield against harm, but as a guiding light toward safety, peace, and freedom.

In every relationship—personal, professional, or spiritual—discernment is a sacred gift. It tunes us to sense when something is amiss, even when everything appears perfectly in place. With humility, we begin to see more clearly. With wisdom, we respond instead of react, stand firm instead of wavering, and choose actions aligned with our deepest good.

One mistake I made early on was assuming others shared my same depth of care. That blindness invited more toxicity than I could have imagined. But as I nurtured discernment, the beauty of authentic connection returned—slowly, surely, like dawn breaking after a long night.

Focusing on Others to Understand Their True Intentions

One overlooked key to discernment is the art of observing others without losing sight of yourself. When you quiet assumptions and silence the noise of your own emotions, you begin to see people as they truly are—not as your hopes or fears would paint them.

Deep listening becomes the fertile soil where discernment takes root. To truly attend to another is to hear not only their words but also the pauses between them to notice the subtle shifts in tone, the language of body and eyes, the emotional currents beneath the surface.

This is not about judgment—it's about love that seeks truth. It doesn't mean absorbing someone else's feelings as your own; it means holding space for their reality without being blinded by it. Discernment listens not to trap someone in deceit, but to uncover the truth that leads to wisdom and freedom.

Ask yourself:

- How do they treat others when nothing can be gained?
- How do they respond when pressure reveals the cracks?
- Do their actions mirror their words—or quietly contradict them?

This practice ties closely to empathy—not the overwhelming kind that erases your own boundaries, but a clear, compassionate understanding. That clarity helps you discern whether words come from sincerity or strategy. When you slow down to notice patterns, you begin to see if a relationship truly nurtures your life—or quietly drains your vitality.

Using Discernment to Guide Conversations

Discernment doesn't stop at spotting red flags—it becomes a steady compass that shapes how you engage. When a conversation shifts toward subtle manipulation, veiled guilt, or quiet coercion, discernment gives you the courage to reset with grace.

Instead of reacting impulsively or retreating in silence, you can respond with calm honesty. You can set boundaries without shame. You can uphold dignity—not just for yourself, but for the other person too.

Scripture reminds us: "Let your conversation be always full of grace, seasoned with salt, so that you may know how to answer everyone"

(Colossians 4:6, NIV). Grace does not soften the truth into weakness—it makes the truth easier to receive, without losing its strength.

Making Wise, Gracious Decisions

Every day brings choices in relationships: to trust or to wait, to go deeper or step away. Discernment guides these decisions intentionally, not impulsively. It pauses the rush of emotion and asks deeper questions: Does this relationship reflect my values? Does it bring peace or confusion? Is it aligned with truth—or merely with comfort?

It reminds us that not every opportunity that glitters is truly good. Proverbs counsels wisely: "The prudent see danger and take refuge, but the simple keep going and pay the penalty" (Proverbs 22:3, NIV). Discernment invites reflection, clarity, and sometimes the courage to walk away.

Over time, discernment builds confidence. It strengthens your ability to hear your inner voice—the Spirit's gentle whisper guiding your steps. The more you listen, the fewer decisions you make from fear, guilt, or insecurity. Instead, your choices begin to flow from peace, wisdom, and self-respect.

Reflection Question

Think back to a recent moment when something felt off in a conversation or relationship. What signs nudged your awareness, and how did you respond? If you could revisit that moment now, how might discernment guide you differently?

Final Thought

Discernment is the quiet art of becoming wise. It is the inner compass that gently shields you and points toward what is true, healthy, and whole. Each time you heed that soft inner nudge and respond with grace, you step more fully into a life of clarity, peace, and integrity.

Over time, those small moments weave together into an extraordinary tapestry: freedom.

"Everyone should be quick to listen, slow to speak, and slow to become angry" (James 1:19, NIV).

Heather and Mike: A Fictional Story of Discernment

Heather and Mike lived in the same apartment complex—close enough for spontaneous moments, yet separate enough to breathe. Over two years, their relationship had deepened like slow-settling roots. They had learned to forgive, to extend grace, to love with more than fleeting feelings.

And yet, a quiet unease lingered. Despite Mike's visible growth—his patience, his thoughtful words—Heather's spirit remained unsettled. She wondered: "Is this the kind of love that will last?"

One evening, as the sun dissolved into the horizon, they walked along the shoreline. The ocean glowed with molten gold. Mike stopped, turned to her, and his voice wavered ever so slightly.

"Heather, I love you more than anything." He hesitated, then pulled a small velvet box from his pocket. "I want to spend the rest of my life with you. Will you marry me?"

It was everything she had pictured—the ocean, the sunset, his steady voice. But her heart tightened, not with joy, but with a quiet ache. Something in her spirit didn't align with his words.

She wanted to smile. To say "yes." To make the moment beautiful. But she couldn't. Not yet.

"Mike," she began carefully, "I care deeply for you. But sometimes I feel like I disappear to keep the peace. I stop bringing up what really matters to me. I shrink so we don't fight. That's not the kind of love I can build a future on."

Mike's face fell, confusion and hurt flickering in his eyes. "So you don't love me?"

"I do," she said softly, "but love isn't just a feeling. It's mutual respect, trust, and understanding. We can't rush this. I need to know we're both whole—individually and together."

She thought of the verse she had prayed countless times over their relationship: "And this is my prayer: that your love may abound more and more in knowledge and depth of insight, so that you may be able to discern what is best" (Philippians 1:9-10, NIV).

Mike looked away, silent for a long moment. Then he said, "I thought doing more for you showed my love. But maybe I haven't really seen you. If you need time, I'll give it. I want to understand."

This wasn't rejection. It was an invitation to something better—truth instead of fantasy, a beginning instead of an ending.

Heather exhaled, the weight of pretending lifting from her chest. "Thank you," she whispered. "I want to take the next step—not because it's expected, but because it's right."

As the last light slipped beneath the waves, they stood together—not at a perfect moment, but at an honest one. A moment grounded in discernment, courage, and a love willing to grow up.

Heather's story isn't just about romance. It's a mirror for every moment we're asked to choose between comfort and truth.

The Banquet Awaits

Discernment is more than protection from harm. It is the quiet doorway leading you beyond the toxic dance—beyond the patterns of fear, guilt, and hidden control that once kept you small.

Each time you pause to listen with love instead of reacting in fear, you step further from the cycles that drained you. You begin to taste what was always meant for you: love that heals rather than hurts, connection that frees rather than confines, wisdom that anchors you in truth.

So what is beyond the toxic dance? Scripture paints the answer this way: "The kingdom of heaven is like a king who prepared a wedding banquet for his son" (Matthew 22:2, NIV). A table where no one competes. Where love flows without condition. Where grace never runs out.

Whether you see this as a glimpse of heaven or simply the deepest longing of the human heart, the invitation is the same: step beyond the toxic dance and closer to a life where love and truth walk hand in hand.

Discernment shows you that you don't have to choose between love and security. There is a way to live where love is secure, and security overflows with love.

This is the beginning of freedom: no longer circling the same painful patterns, no longer silencing your own soul, but moving toward the feast prepared for you—where love and wisdom meet in abundance.

Reflection Question

When facing a pivotal decision in a relationship, how can you pursue wisdom that honors both clarity and love—not only for others, but also for yourself?

Final Thought

Heather didn't walk away from love—she walked deeper into it, guided not by fear or fantasy, but by wisdom. Discernment isn't cold calculation; it's love in action. It listens deeply, sees clearly, and responds with honor.

"If any of you lacks wisdom, you should ask God, who gives generously to all without finding fault, and it will be given to you" (James 1:5, NIV).

You don't have to figure it all out alone. Discernment is love's ally, slowing us down long enough to build something real.

Let love abound in depth and insight. That's the kind worth choosing.

In the last chapter, we explored how discernment allows you to step out of old patterns with clarity and grace. It's the quiet strength that helps you see the truth, even when others won't—*see it yet*.

But healing doesn't stop with you. Every choice you make sends ripples outward. The moment you change your step, the entire dance begins to shift. Some will resist. Some will be inspired. And others will quietly watch, waiting for their own courage to rise.

18

Chapter 11: Spreading the Ripple Effect of Love

Riley had always sensed something was off in her family—an uneasy tension she couldn't name. Yet it wasn't until she stepped away that the full picture snapped into focus: a quiet choreography of repeated patterns, unspoken expectations, and subtle manipulations. She had been dancing a toxic dance she never even realized she was part of.

The rhythm had dictated every step she took. But the moment she chose to break free, the entire sequence began to unravel. What once masqueraded as love or loyalty revealed its true face—fear, obligation, and control disguised as connection.

At first, her choice sparked resistance. Her father branded her selfish. Her mother, torn between love and loyalty, clung to the fragments she could hold. Her siblings scattered—one angry, one quietly supportive, another frozen in uncertainty. Riley knew the cost was high. But she also knew she could never go back.

What surprised her most was the echo her healing created. Over time, her younger sister began to recognize the same patterns Riley had once seen. Inspired by her courage, she too stepped away from dysfunction and began shaping a healthier life. Even Riley's mother, though pressed to conform, found limited ways to stay present.

Not everyone embraced the change—and that was okay. Riley had discovered a liberating truth: healing isn't about controlling others; it's about freeing yourself.

How Your Growth Impacts Those Around You

When one person begins to heal, the dynamics around them inevitably shift. Dysfunction depends on predictable rhythms. When someone stops moving to the old beat, the whole system trembles. Some who thrived in the old patterns resist. Others, hungry for a new way, take notice. Either way, change has begun.

This shift can feel unsettling, even painful. People rarely intend harm—they're just more comfortable with the familiar. Change takes time. But when you hold steady in healthier choices, something remarkable happens: even the most resistant may begin to reflect.

When pushback comes, remember: you don't owe anyone justification for your freedom. A calm, steady, "That no longer works for me," can echo louder than a dozen arguments. Gentle boundaries speak with the greatest strength. People watch. They ponder. And sometimes, watching from a distance, they take their own first step toward healing.

This transformation is beautifully captured in 2 Corinthians 5:17 (NIV): "Therefore, if anyone is in Christ, the new creation has come: the old has gone, the new is here!"

Freedom Day: A Personal Story

My healing began with a single, terrifying decision: to walk away from a business I had co-built with my father. The constant struggle, the quiet manipulation, the slow erosion of peace—it was no longer worth it. Not even a paycheck, not even my investment, could justify one more day in that environment.

The aftermath was exactly what I feared. My father's anger was sharp and cold. My mother, caught in a web of divided loyalty, was discouraged from speaking with me. My sisters responded in different ways—one withdrew, while another quietly chose a path similar to mine. Five people. Five fractured perspectives. A storm of conflict.

At the time, I had two young children, a wife, and a mortgage. Walking away meant no paycheck, no safety net. The only security I carried was the work I had within me—and thankfully, it was enough.

Even amid the tension, my mother found ways to stay connected. Holidays were quieter but lighter. I only asked for her time and nothing more than she could give. I honored the pieces of her love she was able to offer.

Then came a moment that stung like salt in an open wound. I discovered my mother had cashed out her modest retirement to help me. Before I even knew, my father had taken that money and handed it to the employees at the company I left.

The betrayal was deep—but I was already unbound. The chains had broken long before the consequences fully arrived. My father and I didn't speak for years. When we finally did, it was only on the surface. And that was enough.

Because obedience to God often costs more than we expect. It severs ties we once prayed would hold. But it also gives more than we could have imagined: peace, clarity, and a freedom no one else can take away.

I have no regrets. I am healthy. I am free. If I could change one thing, it would be to have written this book sooner, to place a copy in each of their hands. Some might have grown from it. Others might have tossed it aside. But at least I would have known I offered a way forward.

Psychologically, this is the turning point in healing—the moment you stop trying to orchestrate others' freedom and take full responsibility for your own. People may resist, but your peace no longer depends on their response. This is where discernment becomes a safeguard. It allows you to see clearly through the noise of resistance and stay anchored in truth. "And the peace of God, which transcends all understanding, will guard your hearts and your minds in Christ Jesus" (Philippians 4:7, NIV).

The Ripple Effect of Healing

Healing is never confined to one person. It ripples outward. Some will embrace the change. Others will resist it. Some will observe cautiously, waiting for the courage to take their own step. And some may never follow. That's okay.

Your journey isn't about convincing anyone. It's about becoming whole.

In time, even those who resist may soften. They might return with questions, or perhaps with silent gratitude. And some won't. Their choice doesn't diminish the value of yours.

The healthier you become, the brighter your life shines in contrast. Your courage becomes a quiet invitation—a path others may one day walk.

In a family shrouded in shadow, one light can shift the entire atmosphere. Your willingness to heal may be the very contrast someone else needs to believe freedom is possible. This is the beauty of vicarious change: the silent ways your growth plants seeds in others. "In the same way, let your light shine before others, that they may see your good deeds and glorify your Father in heaven" (Matthew 5:16, NIV).

Reflection Question

As you consider your own journey, how might your personal growth indirectly influence those around you—even if they never say a word? Galatians 6:9 (NIV) reminds us: "Let us not become weary in doing good, for at the proper time we will reap a harvest if we do not give up."

Healing takes effort. It often feels thankless in the moment. But every step you take toward truth, peace, and integrity sows seeds you may not see right away. Hold fast. What you plant in courage may bloom in someone else's season.

Final Thought

Transformation is rarely easy, but it is always worth it. The toxic dance ends the moment someone dares to choose freedom. That choice may be misunderstood, resisted, even mocked. But it can quietly inspire others to step out, too.

Healing is a gift—not only to yourself, but to every life your freedom touches. Hold it close. Walk in it. And let its ripples stretch far beyond what you can see.

Is my ripple reaching you? Who will yours reach?

One by one, as we change our steps, a new rhythm begins to rise—not the old dance of fear and control, but the healing cadence of freedom and grace.

Sharing Your Journey: Inviting Others Into Healing

How do you truly help someone? Do you offer quick fixes, shooting from the hip? Or do you bring something deeper—something transformative? It's easy to toss out advice that sounds right in the moment. But true help—the kind that heals and restores—requires more presence, more thought, and above all, more love. Proverbs 25:11 reminds us, "A word aptly spoken is like apples of gold in settings of silver." The right words, spoken at the right time, become a gift—both beautiful and lasting.

Instead of rushing to fix, we're invited to pause and ask: What does this person truly need right now? Not just to feel better, but to become freer, stronger, and more whole.

"You are the light of the world. A town built on a hill cannot be hidden. Neither do people light a lamp and put it under a bowl. Instead, they put it on its stand, and it gives light to everyone in the house. In the same way, let your light shine before others, that they may see your good deeds and glorify your Father in heaven" (Matthew 5:14–16, NIV).

A Seed Planted in Safe Soil—A Fictional Story

The coffee shop buzzed softly with conversation, but Claire barely noticed as she stirred her drink, her mind quietly racing. Across from her sat Melissa, an old friend she hadn't seen in years. Their meeting started light—work, family, the usual small talk. But now, Melissa's eyes glistened as she shared the exhaustion of always trying to fix things, the loneliness of feeling unseen.

Claire hesitated, heart pounding, before reaching into her bag.

"I've been reading something that really helped me see things differently," she said gently, sliding the book across the table. Melissa traced the cover with her fingers, a small, sad smile forming. "*Beyond the Toxic Dance—t*hat is exactly where I need to go."

In that moment, the book was more than just pages and words. It was a quiet, courageous invitation—a symbol of hope, an opening to see life through a new lens. Sharing a book like this—or any resource that speaks truth with grace—isn't about pushing an agenda. It's about extending a hand, offering a doorway to clarity, hope, and healing. It was through a situation just like this that I learned about the ACEs study.

Sharing with Close Relationships: Going Through It Together

Healing often grows strongest when shared with those closest to us—whether a spouse, sibling, best friend, or adult child. Reading together opens doors for conversations that might otherwise feel too fragile to start. It's not just about reading words on a page; it's about creating shared space for growth, understanding, and mutual support.

Psychologically, people process healing best in safe, relational environments. Dr. Sue Johnson, a leading expert in attachment theory, emphasizes that secure connections foster emotional safety—making growth not only possible but sustainable. Reading and discussing together builds bonds and creates a shared language that helps both parties understand each other more deeply.

Inviting someone to read alongside you is inviting them to journey together. If they're hesitant, you might say, "I don't want to pressure you, but this book really changed how I see things, and I'd love to hear your thoughts." And if they're not ready, that's perfectly okay. You've still offered them the gift of healing—no strings attached.

Plowing a Whole Field—A Fictional Story

James and Mitch sat quietly in the break room at the halfway house, discussing the upcoming group meeting. James had been reading through this book and was eager to lead a discussion based on its principles. Mitch shared his excitement but worried about how it might unfold.

"I think *Beyond the Toxic Dance*—this book I've been reading—would really resonate here," James said, leaning back. "People need something relatable and practical. But it's important not to push anyone too hard."

Mitch nodded. "Yeah, many here have walls up. We don't want to rush sharing."

They agreed to keep the group casual and non-pressuring, focusing on healing principles connected to real-life stories. The session would start with open discussion, then break into smaller groups for deeper reflection. Some would share openly; others would listen quietly. The connection felt palpable. Healing happened in vulnerability, shared experience, and compassionate listening. No one tried to fix everything at once—they were simply beginning a journey, walking it together.

Facilitating Group Healing

Group settings provide fertile ground for transformation by creating shared experiences that reduce isolation and foster connection. Whether in community centers, Bible studies, halfway houses, or homes, people find common ground in shared struggles. When they see others walking similar roads, they realize they aren't alone.

Psychologically, group healing thrives on the principle of universality—knowing others share your desires and challenges reduces isolation and builds empathy. Renowned psychiatrist Dr. Irvin Yalom found group dynamics help individuals realize they are not unique, sparking growth, healing, and connection.

There is unique power in community. Witnessing someone else's vulnerability helps us accept our own. Whether in a circle of chairs or over coffee, sharing can make the journey feel less daunting.

Isaiah 58:10 (NIV) reminds us, "If you spend yourselves in behalf of the hungry and satisfy the needs of the oppressed, then your light will rise in the darkness, and your night will become like the noonday."

Healing doesn't only come from professionals; it flourishes in ordinary people showing up with honesty, grace, and Scripture as their guide.

Growth isn't just for ourselves—it becomes brighter when we give it away.

Organizations That Prioritize Healing and Connection

Organizations like shelters, halfway houses, recovery groups, churches, and community centers often seek resources that support relational growth. Sometimes, a resource like *Beyond the Toxic Dance* can give group leaders fresh language for pain and hope—something practical that meets people right where they are, without pretense or pressure.

You don't need to be a therapist or expert to make an impact. A simple conversation with a group leader might open doors to transformation.

Consider approaching a leader with an open invitation: I've been reading this book and thought it might help your group. Would you be open to taking a look? Many leaders seek materials that resonate with their mission. Your offer could provide something fresh and meaningful.

Growth is rarely solo—it echoes louder in community.

Reflection Question

Who in your life might be ready to join you on this adventure, and how can you invite them, offering space for their pace and readiness?

Final Thought

"Therefore confess your sins to each other and pray for each other so that you may be healed. The prayer of a righteous person is powerful and effective" (James 5:16, NIV).

Healing flourishes in community when we open our hearts, share honestly, and support one another with grace. Growth isn't solitary—it's a shared journey that deepens connection and invites transformation.

Transformation spreads when we invite others along. Whether through personal relationships, small groups, or organizations, sharing *Beyond the Toxic Dance* extends the grace that transformed your life. You don't need all the answers or to be an expert. Simply offering the book, a listening ear, and a willingness to walk alongside someone can make all the difference.

This journey isn't about any one book—even *Beyond the Toxic Dance*—it's about the deeper invitation to live freer, love better, and heal more deeply. Whether you use these words, Scripture, or other trusted tools, healing spreads when we pass it on. Simply offering a resource, a listening ear, and a willingness to walk alongside someone can make all the difference.

Using Love to Heal and Influence Others

Jenny had always avoided politics—too much noise, too many arguments, too much division. But when her city faced a crisis, she saw how leadership truly matters. Wise, compassionate leaders brought calm and unity, while manipulative ones thrived on fear and chaos. For the first time, she wondered, "What if discernment applies here too?"

Discernment isn't just for personal relationships; it's essential for choosing the leaders who shape our communities and culture. Scripture reminds us, "When the righteous thrive, the people rejoice; when the wicked rule, the people groan" (Proverbs 29:2, NIV). Psychology echoes this truth: leaders with emotional intelligence and integrity foster trust, safety, and cooperation. Without discernment, we risk empowering those who mask self-interest with charm, charisma, or persuasive slogans.

Political discernment means looking beyond campaign promises and polished sound bites. It prompts deeper, quieter questions:

- Does this leader demonstrate humility, wisdom, and authentic care for others?
- Do their actions align with their words—or shift with convenience?
- Are they motivated by service or self-preservation?

Jesus warned, "Watch out for false prophets. They come to you in sheep's clothing, but inwardly they are ferocious wolves" (Matthew 7:15, NIV). Today, that warning can look like leaders who exploit fear to gain loyalty or manipulate truth to maintain power. A discerning heart notices the signs—empty rhetoric, blame-shifting, a lack of accountability—and instead seeks out those who lead with consistency, compassion, and strength.

A Conversation in Discernment

Ethan and Marcus sat at their usual coffee shop, discussing the upcoming election.

"I really like what Mr. Johnson is saying," Ethan said, scrolling through his phone. "He's promising tax cuts, job growth, and a better future. That's what we need."

Marcus nodded, then paused. "Those are great promises. But have you noticed how he avoids direct questions? He talks a lot about what he'll do, but his past actions don't match his words."

Ethan frowned. "What do you mean?"

"Watch how he handles pressure," Marcus said. "He deflects blame, shifts his position when it benefits him, and uses fear to rally support. That's not leadership—that's control."

"So how do you know which candidates will actually do what they say?"

"I start with their character," Marcus replied. "Do they take responsibility when they fail? Do they treat others with respect, even when no one's watching? Ms. Smith stands for the same political values as Mr. Johnson. She may not have the flashiest campaign, but she quietly shows up for people—even when it costs her. That kind of integrity matters."

Ethan sighed. "It's hard to tell who's real and who's just saying what we want to hear."

"That's why discernment matters," Marcus said. "It's not about who speaks the best or which party they are with. It's about who lives what they say."

Why Discernment Matters in Today's Culture

Discernment doesn't stop with politics. It's just as vital when engaging with media, trends, and cultural narratives. The Apostle Paul encouraged, "Test everything. Hold on to what is good" (1 Thessalonians 5:21, NIV). That call to clarity and courage still applies as we scroll, watch, and absorb messages in a fast-moving, noisy world.

Modern psychology offers a helpful reminder here: confirmation bias. It's our tendency to favor information that confirms our existing beliefs, while dismissing anything that challenges them. Left unchecked, this bias makes us vulnerable to emotionally charged messaging, fear-based appeals, and subtle manipulation. Discernment interrupts this pattern. It gives us the tools to pause, reflect, and search for what's true.

We might ask:

- Is this message rooted in fact or in fear?
- Does it promote love, wisdom, and growth—or division, resentment, and control?
- Does it align with what's timeless and true—or simply echo the loudest voice in the room?

Cultural discernment doesn't mean withdrawing from the world. It means engaging with eyes wide open. It's the strength of someone who sees through the noise and chooses responses grounded in clarity and compassion.

When we live this way, we don't just protect ourselves from deception. We become people who influence the world with wisdom and love.

Reflection Question

When you think about the voices that shape your world—leaders, media, movements—do you discern which ones truly reflect wisdom, humility, and love? What would it look like to listen with both your mind and your heart fully engaged?

Final Thought

Discernment is a skill, a safeguard, and a superpower. Rooted in grace, it helps us navigate complexity with clarity, protect what's good, and influence the world without losing our peace. Whether choosing leaders, filtering cultural messages, or examining our own beliefs, discernment invites us to lead with truth, integrity, and love in action.

Let's look at what love can do among friends next.

A Quiet Movement of Love

It began with four friends who shared the same quiet ache. They were tired—not of faith itself, but of the busyness of life, the surface-level conversations that stayed shallow, and the formality of Sunday routines that often left little room for genuine support. So one evening, instead of attending another program or service, they decided to meet in one another's living rooms.

There was no agenda, no carefully planned curriculum. Just honesty, prayer, and the shared desire to love others well. They started with a simple rhythm—reading a passage of Scripture, sharing where they were struggling, and asking, "How can we help one another live this out?"

As they grew closer, they began to see their community with fresh eyes. Needs became more visible—single parents quietly overwhelmed, neighbors weighed down by grief, families caught in cycles of addiction and shame. Rather than waiting for a program or an official church initiative, they stepped in where they could.

They brought meals, offered rides, babysat for free, sat in hospital waiting rooms, and shared this book with those who were hurting. They didn't see themselves as heroes—just ordinary people choosing to love in practical ways.

And something beautiful happened. As they started reaching out to those who were struggling, some joined them when they met—or formed their own groups. A quiet ripple of healing spread without fanfare or titles, just people choosing presence over performance.

Jesus described this kind of influence when He said, "By this everyone will know that you are my disciples, if you love one another" (John 13:35, NIV). Psychology confirms what Scripture has always shown: relational connection is one of the most powerful forces for healing. Safe, compassionate community rewires our stress responses, lowers shame, and nurtures hope.

Healing doesn't require a platform or a program. It starts with small steps of intentional love.

Practical Next Steps

Here are some sound ideas:

- **Start small.** Invite two or three trusted friends into a conversation about life, faith, and healing. Keep it simple and open.
- **Create space for vulnerability.** Ask questions that go beyond the surface. Listen without rushing to fix or advise.
- **Discuss the ideas or questions in this book.** Let its themes guide your conversations, sparking reflection and deeper dialogue.
- **Extend the ripple.** As you grow together, reach out to someone else who might need support and gently invite them in.

Reflection Question

What would it look like to create a space where love and honesty flow freely—without waiting for someone else to lead the way?

Final Thought

Movements that last rarely start with a crowd. They begin with a few hearts willing to step deeper, love more, and live differently. A quiet gathering in a living room can do more to heal a community than the most polished program.

Who could you invite into a simple, life-giving conversation? The ripple you start may reach farther than you ever imagined.

As we sharpen our discernment in relationships, communities, and culture, we begin to sense something deeper calling us—an invitation to discover the foundational truth beneath it all.

What if the deepest healing, the most lasting freedom, comes not just from wisdom or psychology alone, but from a source uniquely durable and complete?

In the next chapter, we'll explore how the Bible offers that final diagnosis and map—a truth that has stood the test of history and reveals the path to transformation unlike any other.

19

Chapter 12: Discovering the Deepest Truth

You've traveled with me through these pages, walking through gentle truths, honest reflections, and healing invitations. Now, as we arrive at this final stretch of the journey, I want to share something both deeply personal and profoundly hopeful—a truth that has quietly guided everything you've read. It comes from a Scripture that invites both reflection and response: "But in your hearts revere Christ as Lord. Always be prepared to give an answer to everyone who asks you to give the reason for the hope that you have. But do this with gentleness and respect" (1 Peter 3:15, NIV).

This verse isn't just a command; it's a posture—a way of sharing without pressure, without judgment, only with love. I offer it to you as an open hand. This invitation to give an answer is not about winning arguments but about sharing hope rooted in experience and truth. Your beliefs, as always, remain yours.

What History Reveals About Our Struggles to Heal

For much of my life, the Bible was always there—on shelves, in church services, in quiet moments of ritual—but it didn't feel alive. Not until my own healing began did it become something more than words. It became a wellspring of wisdom for forgiveness, restoration, and relational safety. I'm not asking you to see it exactly as I do, but I want to offer you a lens—a way to explore what you may have never considered.

Since humanity's earliest days, we've wrestled with the same question: "How do we live together without breaking each other?" We've tried laws carved in stone, philosophies built on logic, and systems designed for order. Across continents, traditions like Confucianism and Stoicism shaped minds with discipline and reason. But even the best of them missed something essential—gentleness. Space not just for rules, but for grace. Not just order, but transformation.

Despite humanity's best efforts, no philosophy or system has fully addressed the heart's deepest needs—that longing for unconditional love and true belonging.

The Unique Promise of Scripture

This promise challenges us to move beyond surface obedience toward a transformative encounter with God's heart.

When the Torah first appeared—the Bible's earliest writings—it brought an entirely new perspective. These were not just societal rules; they were calls to protect the vulnerable, "leave part of the harvest for the poor, forgive debts every seventh year, and, above all, love your neighbor" (Leviticus 19:18, NIV). Justice intertwined with mercy.

Later, the Dead Sea Scrolls echoed the growing call for integrity and repentance, though grace remained only a whisper on the wind.

Then came Jesus, and with Him, the message of the Bible in its fullness—radiant clarity. Not just behavior modified from the outside, but hearts transformed from within. Teachings that revealed unconditional love, forgiveness even for enemies, and grace powerful enough to heal the deepest wounds.

This was shocking in His time. The religious leaders expected a stricter law; the people wanted political rescue. Instead, Jesus brought something no one saw coming—a love so disarming that it redefined strength itself.

Wisdom Arrived Fully Formed

The Bible's timeless wisdom invites us into a healing journey that psychology can complement but never replace.

Here's what still amazes me: the Bible's wisdom didn't evolve slowly over time. Grace, forgiveness, and Agape love didn't emerge gradually—they appeared fully formed in Jesus' brief ministry, complete, whole, and enduring. As Scripture puts it, "Jesus Christ is the same yesterday and today and forever" (Hebrews 13:8, NIV). Many systems try to shape us from the outside in, focusing on behavior or appearance, but Scripture brings healing from the inside out.

Psychology often tackles struggles one behavior at a time, addressing symptoms more than root causes; meaningful transformation is possible, but it is usually incremental. Even research in attachment theory and relational resilience confirms what Scripture models: lasting change starts with inner security, trust, and love.

By grounding us first in grace, forgiveness, and Agape love, Scripture lays a foundation for relational and emotional wholeness. It shows not just *how* to love, but *whom* to love, creating a ripple that transforms relationships, families, and communities.

Long before psychology studied the healing power of forgiveness, Jesus made it central—not as an option, but as essential nourishment for the soul: "But if you do not forgive others their sins, your Father will not forgive your sins" (Matthew 6:15, NIV).

These are not abstract ideals. They are the architecture of emotional safety and relational restoration.

What Changed—and What Remains

Understanding this helps us appreciate why the Bible remains a vital source for healing even in modern times.

Even after the Bible was complete, the world didn't fully embrace its wisdom. Faith communities treasured its message, but much of humanity continued relying on punishment, hierarchy, and control. Only in recent centuries did psychology begin to explore trauma, early wounds, and the healing power of grace and forgiveness—truths Scripture had already declared.

Why This Matters Today

The Bible's wisdom defies the usual story of progress. It didn't gradually grow into clarity; it began with it. Though written over centuries, the heart of its message—especially in Jesus' ministry—was startlingly clear, radically concise, and remarkably enduring.

It feels given, not discovered. And if it was given, that means its wisdom isn't just ancient—it's living. It still waits for you today, not as a demand, but as an open invitation.

Reflection Question

How could the Bible have spoken with such completeness when modern science is still catching up? And what might shift in your own relationships if you believed this wisdom was already complete?

Final Thought

Across thousands of years, humanity has searched for healing. The most surprising discovery is this: the Bible did not grow into its wisdom. It started with it.

Grace. Forgiveness. Love. Not rules to obey, but invitations to heal. Not rigid demands, but tools for restoration—fresh for every generation.

Durability: Uniqueness and Completeness of Scripture

What if there were something that had endured through every storm of history—unchanged by shifting empires, evolving philosophies, or the rise and fall of human opinion? Something that offers not just fleeting inspiration, but lasting wisdom, hope, and healing for anyone, anywhere, at any time?

Across millennia of cultural upheaval, the Bible has remained a steady beacon. Kingdoms have tried to silence it. Critics have sought to discredit it. Yet it continues to speak—clearer and stronger with every generation—offering a path to wholeness that does not sway with trends or human error.

I'm reminded of my background in chemistry. For centuries, scientists believed the universe was made of four elements: earth, wind, fire, and water. Then came the periodic table, revealing more than a hundred elements and overturning centuries of scientific certainty. Psychology tells a similar story. Freud revolutionized how we think about the mind, yet many of his theories have since been reshaped or discarded. Human understanding evolves; what seemed unshakable yesterday may be obsolete tomorrow.

But the Bible does not behave like a human idea.

It speaks with a timeless clarity that resonates across cultures and centuries. While modern psychology is still uncovering fragments of what makes relationships secure and hearts whole, Scripture named those truths from the very beginning. It is the only source that not only identifies humanity's deepest relational problem—the false tension between safety and love—but also provides the remedy.

This durability is not passive survival but active relevance, continually renewing hope in every generation.

A Personal Word to Skeptics

I understand doubt. I've lived with it. For many, faith has been overshadowed by human failure—leaders who didn't live what they preached, institutions that lost sight of love. But here's the thing: the Bible itself never falters. It doesn't excuse human imperfection; it names it.

"For all have sinned and have fallen short of the glory of God" (Romans 3:23, NIV).

Scripture doesn't gloss over our flaws. It exposes them with honesty, but it doesn't leave us there. It points beyond failure to something sturdier than human effort—grace that cannot be earned, forgiveness that doesn't expire, and love that doesn't shift with time.

I'm not asking you to accept this blindly. I'm simply inviting you to consider: could a wisdom so enduring, so unyielding to time, really be just another human invention? Such honest wrestling honors free will and models the grace at the heart of Scripture itself.

If you want to explore this more deeply, Lee Strobel's *The Case for Christ* offers an honest investigation from the perspective of a former skeptic. His journey might echo parts of your own. Perhaps consider Elon Musk's probability AI calculation of the accuracy of evolution theory. The important part is your willingness to actively seek the truth on your terms without confirmation bias.

Why Durability Matters

The Bible's endurance is more than mere survival. It's relevance. It's reliability. It's transformational power. Human theories age, revise, and fade. Philosophy and science—valuable as they are—live on a shelf life, constantly rewritten as new discoveries emerge. But the Bible remains untouched by those cycles.

Isaiah 40:8 (NIV) says it this way: "The grass withers and the flowers fall, but the word of our God endures forever."

If Scripture were merely human, its ongoing impact would be an anomaly beyond explanation. Plato and Aristotle shaped the world, but their writings have been critiqued and reworked countless times. By contrast, the Bible stands firm, continuing to comfort the brokenhearted, challenge the powerful, and ignite hope for the hopeless—century after century.

Its truths are alive today as they were thousands of years ago. They don't age, because they were never rooted in human limitation. The Bible's enduring presence testifies to its unique role as a foundation for both individual and communal transformation.

In the next sections, we'll look closer at what makes this book unlike any other you've ever encountered. These same truths have already been at work in this journey—quietly shaping, inviting, and offering hope, right where you are.

Reflection Question

What wisdom or truth in your life has remained steady—even as everything else has shifted around you?

Final Thought

God's invitation isn't fragile. It doesn't expire. It's been extended across generations and will outlast every empire, philosophy, and cultural tide.

The Bible is more than a book. It is a living reminder that what God truly desires is relationship.

Durability: Uniqueness and Completeness of Scripture

What if there were something that had endured through every storm of history—unchanged by shifting empires, evolving philosophies, or the rise and fall of human opinion? Something that offers not just fleeting inspiration, but lasting wisdom, hope, and healing for anyone, anywhere, at any time?

Across millennia of cultural upheaval, the Bible has remained a steady beacon. Kingdoms have tried to silence it. Critics have sought to discredit it. Yet it continues to speak—clearer and stronger with every generation—offering a path to wholeness that does not sway with trends or human error.

I'm reminded of my background in chemistry. For centuries, scientists believed the universe was made of four elements: earth, wind, fire, and water. Then came the periodic table, revealing more than a hundred elements and overturning centuries of scientific certainty. Psychology tells a similar story. Freud revolutionized how we think about the mind, yet many of his theories have since been reshaped or discarded. Human understanding evolves; what seemed unshakable yesterday may be obsolete tomorrow.

But the Bible does not behave like a human idea.

It speaks with a timeless clarity that resonates across cultures and centuries. While modern psychology is still uncovering fragments of what makes relationships secure and hearts whole, Scripture named those truths from the very beginning. It is the only source that not only identifies humanity's deepest relational problem—the false tension between safety and love—but also provides the remedy.

This durability is not passive survival but active relevance, continually renewing hope in every generation.

A Personal Word to Skeptics

I understand doubt. I've lived with it. For many, faith has been overshadowed by human failure—leaders who didn't live what they preached, institutions that lost sight of love. But here's the thing: the Bible itself never falters. It doesn't excuse human imperfection; it names it.

"For all have sinned and have fallen short of the glory of God" (Romans 3:23, NIV).

Scripture doesn't gloss over our flaws. It exposes them with honesty, but it doesn't leave us there. It points beyond failure to something sturdier than human effort—grace that cannot be earned, forgiveness that doesn't expire, and love that doesn't shift with time.

I'm not asking you to accept this blindly. I'm simply inviting you to consider: could a wisdom so enduring, so unyielding to time, really be just another human invention? Such honest wrestling honors free will and models the grace at the heart of Scripture itself.

If you want to explore this more deeply, Lee Strobel's *The Case for Christ* offers an honest investigation from the perspective of a former skeptic. His journey might echo parts of your own. Perhaps consider Elon Musk's probability calculation done with AI, concerning the likelihood of evolution theory. Many skeptics have come to faith by earnestly asking God to prove Himself to them in prayer. The important part is your willingness to actively seek the truth on your terms without confirmation bias.

Why Durability Matters

The Bible's endurance is more than mere survival. It's relevance. It's reliability. It's transformational power. Human theories age, revise, and fade. Philosophy and science—valuable as they are—live on a shelf life, constantly rewritten as new discoveries emerge. But the Bible remains untouched by those cycles.

Isaiah 40:8 (NIV) says it this way: "The grass withers and the flowers fall, but the word of our God endures forever."

If Scripture were merely human, its ongoing impact would be an anomaly beyond explanation. Plato and Aristotle shaped the world, but their writings have been critiqued and reworked countless times. By contrast, the Bible stands firm, continuing to comfort the brokenhearted, challenge the powerful, and ignite hope for the hopeless—century after century.

Its truths are alive today as they were thousands of years ago. They don't age, because they were never rooted in human limitation. The Bible's enduring presence testifies to its unique role as a foundation for both individual and communal transformation.

In the next sections, we'll look closer at what makes this book unlike any other you've ever encountered. These same truths have already been at work in this journey—quietly shaping, inviting, and offering hope, right where you are.

Reflection Question

What wisdom or truth in your life has remained steady—even as everything else has shifted around you?

Final Thought

God's invitation isn't fragile. It doesn't expire. It's been extended across generations and will outlast every empire, philosophy, and cultural tide.

The Bible is more than a book. It is a living reminder that what God truly desires is relationship—not rituals, not performance, but connection built on knowing Him and resting in His love. Whether you accept it or not, the invitation remains. It waits.

What Makes This Message Different

"Truly I tell you, anyone who will not receive the kingdom of God like a little child will never enter it."
Luke 18:17 (NIV)

When Jesus walked the earth, He didn't limit His time to the faithful. He shared meals with skeptics, engaged doubters in honest dialogue, and always allowed people to walk away freely. Some followed Him; others didn't. He never forced belief—only extended invitation.

That same gentle invitation has echoed through this book.

Whether you identify as a lifelong believer, a wary skeptic, or someone wounded by religion, you've been invited—not pressured—into a better way. A way of healing that honors both your pain and your agency. Like Jesus Himself, it respects your free will while offering a deeper truth.

As we near the end of this journey, it's time to highlight some of the biggest ideas that have quietly reshaped everything along the way. Others may be found in Appendix C, which are well worth the read. These foundational disruptions haven't just shifted what we think—they've reshaped how we live, relate, and ultimately heal.

These disruptions collectively form a new lens—one that calls us to embrace relationship over rules, love over fear, and transformation over survival.

Disruption 1: Walking with God Is a Relationship, Not a Checklist

Perhaps the biggest shift is the most invisible. You haven't been given a set of rules, spiritual formulas, or religious requirements. Instead, you've been offered a relationship. Not in theory—but through real moments of reflection, awareness, and grace.

Walking with God is not religious performance. It's a relational path.

Scripture says it simply: "He has shown you, O man, what is good. And what does the Lord require of you? To act justly and to love mercy and to walk humbly with your God" (Micah 6:8, NIV). God isn't asking for perfection, but partnership. He wants to walk with you.

This book hasn't asked you to believe perfectly or behave flawlessly. Instead, it has modeled a relational journey with God that grows through honesty, humility, and time. That's how real trust is built.

Skeptics were drawn to Jesus because He didn't rush them. He let them be who they were. Even those who rejected Him were treated with dignity. That kind of love disarms fear and creates space for transformation.

We're not expected to leap into trust. We're invited to take one honest step at a time.

Disruption 2: The Real Binary Choice—Love or Safety

Much of life revolves around an unconscious question: "Do I choose love or safety?"

This book has exposed that false binary. In childhood, many of us learned to sacrifice one for the other. We contorted ourselves to be loved—by performing, pleasing, fixing, or disappearing—or built walls to stay safe through control, distance, or defensiveness.

But God never asked us to choose between love and safety. In Him, we find both. "There is no fear in love. But perfect love drives out fear" (1 John 4:18, NIV). God's love isn't fragile. It doesn't manipulate or abandon. It creates true safety—without conditions or performance.

This shift rewrites how we see our pain and survival. What looked like dysfunction was often survival. Now, survival can give way to real connection built on real love.

The invitation is not to earn love or control safety, but to receive both freely by walking with the One who offers them.

Disruption 3: Narcissists and Empaths Are Co-Villains and Co-Victims

Modern psychology and popular culture often paint narcissists as villains and empaths as victims. It's a tidy story: one abuses, the other absorbs; one manipulates, the other feels too much.

The full picture is more complex—and more freeing.

This book shows narcissists and empaths as mirrors, not opposites. Both develop their patterns to survive a lack of secure love. Narcissists shield vulnerability through control, self-inflation, and distance. Empaths protect theirs with people-pleasing, attunement, and self-erasure.

Both are wounded. Both cause harm. Both need healing.

This doesn't remove accountability—it clarifies it. It frees us from scapegoating one side while ignoring our own roles. It invites everyone, regardless of role, to move from survival to transformation.

Romans 3:23 levels the playing field: "All have sinned and fall short of the glory of God" (NIV). That includes those who harmed us and those we've harmed. Scripture redeems all sinners equally.

Naming narcissists and empaths as co-victims and co-villains creates space for something revolutionary: mutual accountability and grace. It opens a healing path for individuals and relational systems trapped in cycles of blame.

Disruption 4: Grace, Forgiveness, and Love as a New Model for Healing

When old strategies of control, people-pleasing, and withdrawal stop working, what do we do?

We replace them—not with shame or self-discipline—but with something different: grace, forgiveness, and love. These are not soft virtues or optional extras. They are a new internal framework—a spiritual system designed by God for lasting healing. This triad is not theoretical—it's lived reality, accessible to anyone willing to receive it.

Grace is not weakness. It is the ultimate boundary. It offers compassion without co-dependence, safety without enabling. Grace says, "I see what's broken, but it will not define you—or me." Jesus modeled this again and again, protecting dignity while calling people out of sin.

Forgiveness is not denial. It's truth-seeking. It invites us to reexamine what happened, what it meant, and how it shaped us. Forgiveness isn't pretending it didn't hurt; it's choosing to move forward in truth, releasing resentment because God's justice surpasses ours.

Love—especially Agape love—is action, not just feeling. It listens deeply, honors the image of God in others, and reconnects what shame and fear have shattered. "Above all, love each other deeply, because love covers over a multitude of sins" (1 Peter 4:8, NIV).

Together, grace, forgiveness, and love form a self-reinforcing system. They create an internal environment where shame cannot survive, blame loses power, and manipulation dissolves. They protect what matters most:

relationship, reality, and restoration.

This triad is disruptive because it works—not just feeling good but producing fruit. As Paul wrote, "Be transformed by the renewing of your mind" (Romans 12:2, NIV). This renewal happens not by force, but by realigning beliefs, responses, and relationships with God's truth.

Disruption 5: Experience Validates the Truth

This book hasn't just told you what's true. It has shown you. Through stories, reflections, and your own engagement, truth is taking root—not just in your mind but in your heart and habits.

That's epistemology—how we know what we know.

Next, we'll explore why the Bible isn't just a helpful guide, but the only enduring source of complete healing. But before that, consider this: the best proof of truth isn't theological argument—it's a changed life.

Jesus said, "Wisdom is proved right by her children" (Luke 7:35, NIV). We know the tree by its fruit. If this journey has made you more whole, honest, and loving—that is no coincidence. It is the fruit of walking in truth.

Healing becomes real—not through coercion—but through experience. Through choosing truth—and watching it work. True knowledge comes from lived experience, and this book invites you to test these truths in your own life.

Reflection Question

Which of these foundational disruptions has shifted how you see yourself or others? What would it look like to walk that out in one relationship this week?

Final Thought

Jesus never demanded belief as a condition for compassion. He simply walked with people, invited trust, and let the fruit speak for itself.

That invitation stands today.

You've encountered a different way to see yourself, others, and God—not through shame or fear, but through clarity, love, and truth.

Now, with this foundation, we're ready for one final step: discovering why Scripture isn't just part of healing—it's the source.

It's not flashy or performative—but deeply, quietly powerful.

The Final Diagnosis, the True Map

In a world of shifting truths, the Bible offers a steady path—not by commanding compliance but by inviting trust rooted in lived relationship.

Every healing journey eventually confronts a core question: "What can I actually trust?" After all the books, therapy sessions, and painful life lessons, what remains as a reliable compass when emotions are foggy, the heart is weary, and the mind is conflicted?

This question isn't theoretical—it's the hinge of our lives. It determines not only where we look for answers, but whether we trust any answers at all. In the search for identity, healing, and wholeness, people often collect a patchwork of tools: psychology, self-help, spirituality, advice from mentors, Instagram quotes, TED Talks. Some offer real help. Others deepen the confusion. But none of them, standing alone or stitched together, can do what the Bible does.

This is the ultimate disruption: the Bible is not merely helpful—it is complete. It is not merely wise—it is timeless. It is not merely a book—it is the only enduring map for real transformation, grounded in truth and secured by love.

More Than Moral Advice

For many, especially those raised around religion, the Bible is familiar but misunderstood. Its verses are often heard as commands, reduced to rules, or twisted into judgment. What they may not have seen is its extraordinary depth: its diagnosis of the human heart, its blueprint for relationships, its clarity about manipulation, pride, shame, addiction, fear, false identities, and fragile coping strategies.

You don't need a PhD to notice: Scripture describes narcissism long before modern psychology named it. It warns against manipulation, self-exaltation, false humility, flattery, and hypocrisy. It also calls out enmeshment, idolatry, people-pleasing, and the pain of over-functioning—patterns we now recognize as classic empath dynamics. These behaviors are not new. They're ancient, deeply human survival strategies in a fallen world.

But the Bible doesn't stop at naming the disease. It offers the cure.

From Genesis to Revelation, it reveals a love that is secure, not conditional. It invites us into a journey of relational healing—not moral performance. It tells the story of a God who walks with broken people—not because they've earned it, but because He loves them. And it offers a complete triad for transformation: grace, forgiveness, and love.

Why This Is Disruptive

This may not seem radical to someone who has walked with God for years. But to a modern audience shaped by therapy culture, religious trauma, and skepticism, it cuts against the grain. The dominant worldview today suggests:

- Truth is subjective.
- Healing is self-directed.
- Scripture is outdated or oppressive.
- Transformation comes from within—or not at all.

But this book—and perhaps your journey through it—has exposed a deeper reality: we need more than self. When the self is wounded, blind, or defensive, it cannot heal itself. When truth shifts with emotion or culture, it offers no anchor. When love depends on performance, it never feels secure.

Only Scripture offers what modern frameworks cannot: a love that tells the truth, a truth that leads to transformation, and a path that never changes—because it's built on the eternal nature of God.

As Hebrews 13:8 reminds us, "Jesus Christ is the same yesterday and today and forever." Like Him, the love, forgiveness, and grace described in Scripture are unchanging—retroactive love through forgiveness, love in real time through grace, and Agape love forevermore.

As Jesus said, "If you hold to my teaching, you are really my disciples. Then you will know the truth, and the truth will set you free" (John 8:31–32, NIV).

Walking with God: A Real Map, Not a Metaphor

In the previous section, we explored the idea of walking with God as a lived relationship—not a religious concept, but a way of life marked by daily alignment, trust, and conversation. What makes that walk possible is the reliability of the One we're walking with—and the map He's given us.

Unlike therapy models that adjust with trends or philosophies that evolve with culture, Scripture doesn't change. It doesn't get updated or rebranded. It remains relevant because it reflects the unchanging design of human nature and the consistent character of God.

It also speaks to skeptics. Throughout Jesus' ministry, doubters were not excluded—they were invited. Thomas wasn't rejected for questioning. The Pharisee Nicodemus came to Jesus at night with curiosity, not certainty. The rich young ruler walked away sorrowful, but not coerced. Free will was honored then, just as it is now. The Bible welcomes questions, but it also claims authority—not by force, but by fruit. As Jesus said, "Wisdom is proved right by her children" (Luke 7:35, NIV).

The Map in Action: Grace, Forgiveness, and Love

If you've seen anything clearly by now, it's this: the triad of grace, forgiveness, and love isn't a list of nice ideas. It's a full system for living, relating, and healing. It works because it flows directly from God's character and is fully revealed in Scripture.

Grace gives us safety without compromise. It is not permissiveness. It is the firm and loving boundary that says: "You matter, and so do I." It welcomes truth while protecting dignity. It creates the container where healing can happen.

Forgiveness reclaims the truth. It reframes not by denial, but by clarity—naming what happened, releasing vengeance, and seeing the image of God in the offender without denying harm. It is not weakness; it is power with peace.

Love, in its biblical form—Agape—is not mere affection. It is active commitment. It listens deeply, tells the truth gently, and moves toward others with courage. This love transforms not only relationships but entire systems.

Together, these three form a complete strategy that exposes the toxic cycle of shame, blame, denial, performance, and control. They do what self-help can't do: they reach the root of the human condition.

They are not just therapy. They are truth. They are Jesus in action.

As a simple next step, try choosing one relationship where you can practice offering grace, forgiveness, or love in a new way. What changes?

Reflection Question

What part of your current healing journey feels incomplete, and how might embracing the Bible's enduring wisdom—its grace, forgiveness, and love—offer a more lasting transformation?

Final Thought: Why This Map Endures

The Bible endures not because it's old, but because it's true. It doesn't need to evolve to stay relevant—because humans haven't evolved out of their need for love, security, truth, and transformation. We are still, as ever, in need of a Savior. And that Savior is still inviting us to walk with Him. Grace, forgiveness, and love are how God treats us and, made in His image, how we are to treat each other.

If this journey has sparked something in you, let it continue:

Not by willpower, but by walking.
Not by fixing, but by following.
Not by striving, but by surrender.

You don't need to write your own map.
The map already exists.
And the One who wrote it is walking with you.
All are welcome.

Poetic Reflection and Epilogue: Coming Home

"Here I am! I stand at the door and knock.
If anyone hears my voice and opens the door,
I will come in and eat with that person, and they with me."
Revelation 3:20, NIV

On the other side of that door,
I found arms that never let go,
a whisper that called me beloved,
a peace I had never known.

I stepped through,
and I was finally home.

Now I step aside and point you to Him—
the One who is still knocking,
still welcoming,
still waiting.

It's your choice.

Keep walking with Him.

Tools for Transformation

When I was a child, a close friend had a strategic advantage in his house. Around one corner, a small mirror allowed him to see anyone approaching before they could see him. He would wait silently, watching me walk toward him, then at the last possible moment leap out and shout, "BOO!" It worked every time.

Eventually, I discovered the mirror.

The game changed the moment I understood how he always seemed one step ahead. Knowledge did not remove the corner. It removed the surprise.

That simple prank carries a lasting truth: when you know what to expect, you are no longer easily trapped.

The appendices that follow—A, B, and C—are designed to give you that mirror.

I considered placing this material in earlier chapters because it is foundational. Instead, I gathered it here in concentrated form so you can engage it deliberately and return to it repeatedly. These pages are not supplemental. They are structural.

They are designed to elevate your discernment—your emotional intelligence, if you prefer that language—but more than that, your capacity to see clearly. Discernment is not suspicion. It is trained perception. It is the ability to recognize patterns before they fully unfold.

Scripture describes maturity this way: "Solid food is for the mature, for those who have their powers of discernment trained by constant practice to distinguish good from evil" (Hebrews 5:14). Discernment is not accidental. It is trained. And training requires repetition.

You do not need to memorize these pages word-for-word. But you do need to internalize them at an applied level.

You might begin by identifying the techniques most often used against you and study those first. Or you might track which techniques you personally tend to use and acknowledge the quiet fear that triggers those moments. Growth requires honesty in both directions. How you approach the material can be adapted to your needs—but engaging it consistently is essential.

At minimum, I recommend reading through Appendices A and B each night before sleep for approximately two weeks. Repetition strengthens recognition. Recognition strengthens clarity. Clarity strengthens freedom.

After that, return to them periodically as reinforcement.

Appendix C is different. It is not supplemental. It is the concentrated crystallization of the 20+ foundational disruptions woven throughout this book—the hidden framework behind every pattern, story, and insight you have encountered. It names the distortions that quietly shape behavior, thought, and expectation. It trains you to see them clearly before they harden into belief. Exposure to these disruptions recalibrates your perception. When your mind becomes accustomed to truth, distortion loses its power.

The more familiar you become with these patterns and disruptions, the less reactive you will be. What once felt confusing will begin to feel predictable. What once felt powerful will begin to feel small.

And what becomes visible—through disciplined observation, reflection, and practice—loses its quiet control. You cannot eliminate every corner, but with disciplined practice and trained discernment, you can learn to see around them—and in that clarity, freedom becomes real.

Appendix A: 25 Traits of Narcissistic Control

Recognizing and Responding with Truth and Love

This section highlights traits commonly seen in people who rely on control to protect a fragile sense of self. Whether or not someone has a formal diagnosis, these behaviors can still cause pain in everyday relationships. Recognizing the patterns is not about labeling others. We do this to equip ourselves to respond in ways that protect our peace, strengthen our integrity, and open the door to truth and love.

In my adventures, I found being prepared, as this appendix assists, smooths out those potentially awkward moments of healing. I could engage these ideas at will in real time. This disrupted the toxicity and cleansed the relationship with a powerful healing ointment. A medical professional is prepared before the emergency, and similarly you are encouraged to be prepared for relationships' difficult moments.

Each entry includes a clear description, a gracious response you might offer when facing this behavior, and a verse from the Bible to anchor your heart in deeper wisdom. Even when relationships feel difficult or confusing, you are not alone and there is always a way forward.

Discerning Traits That Matter

Learn to recognize these patterns so you can respond with truth and love.

1. Superiority Complex (Arrogance)

Description: An inflated sense of self-importance that often shows up as condescension, entitlement, or the belief that others don't measure up.

Possible Grace: "I understand you believe you are important. I agree and I am too. I believe each of us contributes something that matters."

Bible: "For those who exalt themselves will be humbled, and those who humble themselves will be exalted" (Matthew 23:12, NIV).

Know / Not My Situation (circle one)

* * *

2. Entitlement

Description: A belief that they deserve special treatment, privileges, or recognition often without regard for effort, fairness, or others' needs.

Possible Grace: "We all deserve to be treated fairly, and I believe everyone should contribute to the shared good."

Bible: "Do nothing out of selfish ambition or vain conceit. Rather, in humility value others above yourselves" (Philippians 2:3, NIV).

Know / Not My Situation (circle one)

* * *

3. Exaggerated Need for Admiration

Description: Constantly seeking praise or validation in order to soothe an inner insecurity, often at the expense of mutual connection.

Possible Grace: "I appreciate your efforts, but we all need to work together for mutual success."

Bible: "Let someone else praise you, and not your own mouth; an outsider, and not your own lips" (Proverbs 27:2, NIV).

Know / Not My Situation (circle one)

* * *

4. Manipulative and Exploitative

Description: Using others to serve their own interests, whether through guilt, deceit, pressure, or subtle power plays.

Possible Grace: "I value honest relationships where mutual respect is key to moving forward."

Bible: "The integrity of the upright guides them, but the unfaithful are destroyed by their duplicity" (Proverbs 11:3, NIV).

Know / Not My Situation (circle one)

* * *

5. Lack of Empathy

Description: A persistent inability or unwillingness to understand or care about another person's feelings or experiences.

Possible Grace: "I recognize we may see this differently, but I think it's important that we listen to each other."

Bible: "Rejoice with those who rejoice; mourn with those who mourn" (Romans 12:15, NIV).

Know / Not My Situation (circle one)

* * *

6. Deceptiveness

Description: Habitually twisting facts, withholding truth, or presenting false information to control how others perceive reality.

Possible Grace: "I believe honesty is essential for trust. Without it, we can't build something lasting."

Bible: "The Lord detests lying lips, but he delights in people who are trustworthy" (Proverbs 12:22, NIV).

Know / Not My Situation (circle one)

* * *

7. Interrupting & Over-Speaking

Description: Taking over conversations, speaking over others, or steering dialogue to maintain control or superiority.

Possible Grace: "I'd love to hear your thoughts too. Let's make sure everyone has space to share."

Bible: "Everyone should be quick to listen, slow to speak and slow to become angry" (James 1:19, NIV).

Know / Not My Situation (circle one)

* * *

8. Blame-Shifting

Description: Refusing to take ownership for mistakes, instead redirecting blame to others often subtly or through deflection.

Possible Grace: "We all play a role in what happens. It matters that we own our part with honesty."

Bible: "Whoever conceals their sins does not prosper, but the one who confesses and renounces them finds mercy" (Proverbs 28:13, NIV).

Know / Not My Situation (circle one)

* * *

9. Victimization

Description: Regularly casting themselves as the injured party—even when they've caused harm—in order to avoid accountability or gain sympathy.

Possible Grace: "I know hard things happen. But moving forward takes honesty, not blame."

Bible: "Each of us will give an account of ourselves to God" (Romans 14:12, NIV).

Know / Not My Situation (circle one)

* * *

10. Disregard for Boundaries

Description: Ignoring or pushing past the emotional, physical, or relational limits others set—often without apology.

Possible Grace: "I respect your limits, and I ask that you respect mine as well."

Bible: "Do not move an ancient boundary stone set up by your ancestors" (Proverbs 22:28, NIV).

Know / Not My Situation (circle one)

* * *

11. Vindictive and Unforgiving

Description: Seeking revenge and holding grudges long after wrongs have been committed.

Possible Grace: "Forgiveness brings peace, and I choose to release any anger or resentment."

Bible: "But if you do not forgive others their trespasses, neither will your Father forgive your trespasses" (Matthew 6:15, NIV).

Know / Not My Situation (circle one)

* * *

12. Passive-Aggressiveness

Description: Expressing hostility indirectly through sarcasm, backhanded compliments, or subtle insults.

Possible Grace: "Let's be honest with each other. Open communication helps us both."

Bible: "Do not let any unwholesome talk come out of your mouths, but only what is helpful for building others up according to their needs, that it may benefit those who listen" (Ephesians 4:29, NIV).

Know / Not My Situation (circle one)

* * *

13. Gaslighting

Description: Manipulating someone into doubting their own reality or sanity.

Possible Grace: "I trust my perception, and I believe in addressing matters with clarity and truth."

Bible: "You will know the truth, and the truth will set you free" (John 8:32, NIV).

Know / Not My Situation (circle one)

* * *

14. Grandiosity

Description: An exaggerated sense of self-importance, expecting admiration and deference from others.

Possible Grace: "We all have unique strengths, and I believe every person has something valuable to contribute."

Bible: "If anyone thinks they are something when they are not, they deceive themselves" (Galatians 6:3, NIV).

Know / Not My Situation (circle one)

* * *

15. Jealousy and Envy

Description: Resentment of others' success or a fear of losing what they have.

Possible Grace: "I celebrate your success, and I trust that there is enough for all of us."

Bible: "For where jealousy and selfish ambition exist, there will be disorder and every vile practice" (James 3:16, NIV).

Know / Not My Situation (circle one)

* * *

16. Hyper-Criticism

Description: Constantly criticizing others while ignoring their own faults.

Possible Grace: "Let's focus on constructive feedback and support each other in growth."

Bible: "Why do you see the speck that is in your brother's eye, but do not notice the log that is in your own eye?" (Matthew 7:3, NIV).

Know / Not My Situation (circle one)

* * *

17. Rage

Description: Explosive anger when challenged, criticized, or denied something they want.

Possible Grace: "I understand you're upset, but let's try to address this calmly and with understanding."

Bible: "In your anger do not sin: Do not let the sun go down while you are still angry" (Ephesians 4:26, NIV).

Know / Not My Situation (circle one)

* * *

18. Entitlement to Loyalty

Description: Expecting blind loyalty, regardless of their behavior or actions.

Possible Grace: True loyalty is mutual, and it must be based on respect and trust.

Bible: "For am I now seeking the approval of man, or of God? Or am I trying to please man? If I were still trying to please man, I would not be a servant of Christ" (Galatians 1:10, NIV).

Know / Not My Situation (circle one)

* * *

19. Coldness and Emotional Withholding

Description: Withdrawing affection or warmth as a form of control or punishment.

Possible Grace: "I value emotional honesty, and I believe in connecting heart-to-heart."

Bible: "Let all bitterness and wrath and anger and clamor and slander be put away from you, along with all malice" (Ephesians 4:31, NIV).

Know / Not My Situation (circle one)

* * *

20. Shaming and Belittling

Description: Using humiliation or insults to make others feel inferior or insecure.

Possible Grace: "We all deserve respect, and it's important to speak with kindness and dignity."

Bible: "Whoever mocks the poor shows contempt for their Maker; whoever gloats over disaster will not go unpunished" (Proverbs 17:5, NIV).

Know / Not My Situation (circle one)

* * *

21. Projection

Description: Accusing others of the very faults or behaviors they refuse to acknowledge in themselves.

Possible Grace: "Let's focus on addressing the issue at hand rather than pointing fingers."

Bible: "For with the judgment you pronounce, you will be judged, and with the measure you use, it will be measured to you" (Matthew 7:2, NIV).

Know / Not My Situation (circle one)

* * *

22. Over-Competitiveness

Description: Viewing relationships and interactions as a constant competition where one must always win.

Possible Grace: "I believe we can succeed together, and collaboration brings the best results."

Bible: "The one who is least among you all is the one who is great" (Luke 9:48, NIV).

Know / Not My Situation (circle one)

* * *

23. Lack of Accountability

Description: Never admitting wrongdoing or mistakes, and often shifting blame to others.

Possible Grace: "I believe that we all grow when we own our mistakes and learn from them."

Bible: "Whoever conceals their sins does not prosper, but the one who confesses and renounces them finds mercy" (Proverbs 28:13, NIV).

Know / Not My Situation (circle one)

24. Unpredictability

Description: Engaging in erratic behavior, often making others feel uneasy or on edge.

Possible Grace: "I value consistency and predictability in relationships, and it helps build trust."

Bible: "For God is not a God of confusion but of peace" (1 Corinthians 14:33, NIV).

Know / Not My Situation (circle one)

* * *

25. Constant Drama

Description: Creating or amplifying problems, conflicts, or crises in order to remain the center of attention.

Possible Grace: "Let's work together to keep things calm and focused on solutions."

Bible: "The fruit of the Spirit is love, joy, peace, forbearance, kindness, goodness, faithfulness, gentleness, and self-control" (Galatians 5:22–23, NIV).

Know / Not My Situation (circle one)

* * *

The Plug-In Effect: A Personal Story

I once had a conversation with someone whose behavior had confused and hurt me for years. Every time I peacefully named a tactic—triangulation, guilt, blame-shifting—they'd instantly stop using it. But within days, a new one would appear, as if downloaded from some invisible menu. I started to notice the pattern. When one plug-in failed, another one loaded.

At first, I braced for battle each time. But over time, I realized something deeper: the moment I stopped reacting and started standing firm, something shifted. The power behind the plug-ins began to weaken. Not because I confronted everything at once—but because I stayed consistent and calm, letting time and truth do their work.

Control, it turns out, doesn't need a dramatic showdown to lose its grip. You don't have to unplug every tactic in a single conversation. Just recognize the pattern, set one gracious boundary at a time, and give space for what's real to surface. Grace provides both the love and security needed for healthy growth if they choose.

You're not responsible for changing the other person. You're simply invited to protect what's true in you.

Appendix B: 10 Common Types of Narcissistic Personalities

Costumes of Control and How to See Through Them

You are welcome to start digesting this Appendix before Chapter 9. But to use this section really well, it's important to keep working your way through the rest of the book—at least through the end of Chapter 9. That journey lays the foundation you need: the sincerity, emotional clarity, and spiritual grounding that give you the wisdom to use what's here in a way that brings healing, not harm.

You Will Know Them By Their Costumes

What you'll find here isn't a verdict on a person's entire identity—it's a snapshot of the emotional costume they may be wearing. Narcissists often avoid vulnerability at all costs. So what you see—the behaviors, the personas—isn't the real person. It's a carefully crafted mask meant to protect a fragile self and keep others at a safe emotional distance. These narcissistic costumes reflect deeper spiritual bondage or distortions of God-given identity.

That's why it's helpful to think of these types as costumes. Sometimes, the patterns are easier to spot than the deeper traits hiding underneath. Recognizing the type helps you decode what's really going on. When you understand the costume, you can also name the tools they use—and quietly take them out of play.

The real power of this Appendix is twofold:

- It helps you spot patterns quickly, so you see the big picture and don't get stuck in ever-shifting details.
- This Appendix helps you see where to gently apply grace and love into the pattern and hopefully find the real person behind it.

The costumes tend to be carefully knit and held together with minimal thread. Once you realize that only a few traits hold the whole pattern together, you can focus your energy where it counts—setting boundaries around what matters and refusing to give away your peace. This shrinks the job dramatically. Discerning costumes builds not only personal peace but social trust.

While I was writing this Appendix, I encountered a spiritual narcissist—someone who had weaponized a well-known theological debate to gain control. He had clearly studied the issue in depth and came prepared, armed with arguments and ready to present himself as the final authority.

Anyone who stepped into the debate found themselves outmatched—not because they lacked faith, but because they weren't prepared for the trap. He had just enough conversational finesse to keep circling everything back to that one narrow topic, using it to block genuine connection and inflate the issue from a minor esoteric disagreement into what he claimed was the ultimate measure of biblical truth.

But I wasn't going to walk into that trap. I simply acknowledged that the issue was clearly important to him—and then gently shared that it held no weight for my own faith or spiritual life. That one response stopped him cold. With his chosen weapon disarmed, there was nothing left to sustain the mask. And just like that, the performance fell flat.

This is the kind of freedom this section is meant to offer. When you understand the costume—and its limitations—you can respond with grace, strength, and clarity. Let this guide be armor for your peace—and a quiet invitation to live unmasked, even when others refuse to. What costumes will be at your dance?

When you can see the patterns clearly, you stop feeling like you're dancing blindfolded. You start to notice where the rhythm repeats—and where you can step away from the pull. This awareness doesn't just protect you; it frees you to choose a different tempo, one grounded in truth and grace.

1. Grandiose Narcissist

Some masks are easy to spot. These are the showier types—the ones who crave the spotlight and often wear their need for admiration out loud.

Mask Description: The grandiose narcissist is the most visible and classic form of narcissism. They are confident, attention-seeking, and demand admiration from others. Their sense of self-worth is built on being perceived as superior and special, and they openly display their need for recognition.

Costume Details:

- Highly confident, often bordering on arrogance.
- Frequently boasts about their achievements, talents, or status.
- Expects special treatment and feels entitled to it.
- Struggles with empathy, often disregarding the feelings of others.
- Seeks constant validation and admiration from others.

Psychological Insights: Grandiose narcissists often possess fragile self-esteem hidden behind their outward grandiosity. Their constant need for attention and validation reflects deep insecurities. However, they may not recognize the impact of their behaviors on others due to their self-centered focus.

Biblical Perspective: Proverbs 16:18 warns that pride comes before destruction, and Philippians 2:3–4 encourages humility, putting the needs of others before our own—a direct challenge to the grandiose narcissist's self-focus.

Grace consideration: Appealing to their desire to be seen, while gently expanding the spotlight to include others. When you model shared value and invite inclusive participation, it can deflate their need to dominate without direct confrontation.

2. Vulnerable Narcissist

Other narcissists hide behind shadows. They may not seem demanding at first—but they quietly draw power through sympathy, guilt, or emotional dependence.

Description: Vulnerable narcissists present a more passive form of narcissism. Rather than openly seeking admiration, they tend to play the victim and look for sympathy. Their narcissism is less obvious but still rooted in a deep need for validation and recognition.

Costume Details:

- Appears shy, self-deprecating, or withdrawn.
- Seeks sympathy and attention by presenting themselves as victims.
- Highly sensitive to criticism, often reacting with anger or hurt.
- Struggles to take responsibility for their actions, often blaming others.
- Feels misunderstood and often uses passive-aggressive behavior to manipulate others.

Psychological Insights: Covert narcissists often experience significant emotional distress, struggling with feelings of inadequacy that are masked by their victim mentality. Their passive-aggressive tactics are an attempt to manipulate others into providing them with the validation they crave.

Biblical Perspective: The Bible teaches that we should not seek pity but instead encourage one another (Galatians 6:2). It also cautions against murmuring and complaining, as seen in Philippians 2:14–15, which counters the covert narcissist's tendency toward passive resistance.

Gracious consideration: Staying grounded in your own sense of peace, without getting pulled into their emotional fog. Their power fades when you gently affirm their humanity but don't over-invest in rescuing, defending, or explaining yourself.

Vulnerability without humility becomes a trap, not a bridge. When someone clings to pain as proof of worth, it's a mask that invites endless rescue attempts. But grace doesn't fuel the mask—it waits patiently for the person beneath it to breathe.

3. Spiritual Narcissist

This next type is especially confusing—and deeply painful for many. When someone uses faith as a weapon, the harm cuts deeper than logic can reach.

Description: Spiritual narcissists use their religious or spiritual beliefs to elevate themselves above others. They present themselves as morally superior or more enlightened, often using their knowledge of spirituality to gain admiration or manipulate others into believing they are on a higher spiritual plane.

Costume Details:

- Uses spirituality or religious knowledge to gain social status.
- Believes they are morally or spiritually superior to others.
- Can manipulate others by exploiting religious or spiritual authority.
- Often judges others harshly, believing their own spiritual practices make them more righteous.
- May appear humble on the surface but uses spirituality as a way to control and dominate.

Psychological Insights: Spiritual narcissists often have deep insecurities, which they attempt to cover by projecting a false sense of spiritual superiority. Their narcissism manifests in a belief that they are entitled to divine favor and use their perceived higher status to control others, all while hiding their true vulnerabilities.

Biblical Perspective: Jesus cautioned against prideful religious practices in Matthew 23:5–7, calling out those who outwardly appear righteous but are inwardly self-serving. Philippians 2:3–4 teaches that true humility, rooted in servitude and the interest of others, is a hallmark of spiritual maturity—something spiritual narcissists often miss.

Grace consideration: Letting your quiet confidence speak for itself. When you refuse to engage in power struggles over doctrine or righteousness, and instead walk in love and humility, their need to be right loses traction.

It can feel disorienting when faith is used as a weapon. But even here, love isn't powerless. Real faith doesn't compete—it simply shines, steady and unthreatened, like a lighthouse cutting through stormy debate.

4. Cerebral Narcissist

Some people impress with how much they know—but behind all the facts and theories, something feels off. Conversations become one-sided. Insight becomes control. Their intellect isn't a bridge to others—it's a barrier.

Description: Cerebral narcissists place their value on intellect and often seek admiration for their intelligence. They believe that their intelligence or knowledge makes them superior to others and can often belittle or look down on those they consider less knowledgeable.

Costume Details:

- Highly intellectual, often dismissive of others' ideas or opinions.
- Seeks admiration for their knowledge or intellect.
- May boast about their education, accomplishments, or intellectual abilities.
- Dismisses others' perspectives, believing they are more enlightened or smarter.
- Can be condescending or sarcastic in their interactions with others.

Psychological Insights: Cerebral narcissists often feel threatened by the intelligence of others, as their self-worth is tied to being seen as intellectually superior. This type of narcissist may isolate themselves with those they consider intelligent to maintain their sense of dominance.

Biblical Perspective: 1 Corinthians 8:1–3 emphasizes that knowledge can lead to arrogance if not balanced with love, urging believers to seek understanding with humility. Proverbs 3:13–18 highlights that true wisdom comes from God, not from human intellect alone.

Grace consideration: Responding with curiosity rather than competition. By acknowledging their intellect without shrinking back or trying to match it, you protect your own clarity—and subtly remind them that wisdom is more than just knowledge.

Intelligence, like any gift, can either build walls or build bridges. The difference lies not in how much someone knows, but in how willing they are to love beyond knowing.

* * *

We've looked *at some of the more visible or spiritually confusing patterns—now let's walk through the rest of the costumes, which may be subtler but are just as important. These remaining masks may not always look loud, but their impact can be just as steady. Sometimes it's the quiet costumes—those stitched from kindness or humility—that hide the deepest threads of control.*

* * *

5. Malignant Narcissist

This type is rare, but devastating. When cruelty and narcissism combine, the result isn't just self-centeredness—it's calculated harm.

Description: Malignant narcissism is the most toxic and dangerous form of narcissism. This type combines elements of narcissistic personality disorder with antisocial traits, including aggression, a desire for power, and a lack of empathy. Malignant narcissists may be manipulative, abusive, and destructive to those around them.

Costume Details:

- Exhibits a profound lack of empathy, often engaging in cruel or abusive behavior.
- Has a deep desire for power and control, often using manipulation or deceit.
- May show signs of aggression or even sadism.
- Feels entitled to harm others to get what they want.
- May lack remorse for their actions and show no regard for others' well-being.

Psychological Insights: Malignant narcissists are often driven by a need to dominate and manipulate others, viewing people as tools to be used for personal gain. Their behaviors may include gaslighting, emotional abuse, and coercion. Their lack of empathy is a hallmark of their pathology, making them particularly dangerous in relationships.

Biblical Perspective: Malignant narcissism goes against the Biblical principle of loving others as ourselves (Mark 12:31). Romans 13:10 teaches that love does no harm to a neighbor, a clear contrast to the behaviors exhibited by malignant narcissists.

Grace consideration: Prioritizing your safety—emotionally, spiritually, and physically—above staying in relationship. Their weakness lies in being exposed, not in lacking empathy. Calmly refusing to play their game protects your peace and robs them of power.

6. Communal Narcissist

This next type often hides behind service. They seem selfless—but the real goal isn't helping. It's being seen helping.

Description: Communal narcissists gain admiration and validation by positioning themselves as selfless or caring, often working in social causes or professions that help others. They use their good deeds to gain praise and attention, but their primary focus is on how others perceive them.

Costume Details:

- Frequently involved in charitable work or helping others.
- Seeks admiration for their "goodness" or selflessness.
- Enjoys being seen as the hero or savior.
- May use altruistic acts to manipulate others into feeling indebted.
- Often projects an image of humility while seeking constant recognition.

Psychological Insights: Communal narcissists use helping behaviors to feed their ego, often seeking validation through their selfless actions. The focus on public recognition can undermine genuine compassion and may make their actions more about themselves than the people they claim to help.

Biblical Perspective: Matthew 6:1–4 advises against practicing righteousness for public recognition, emphasizing that true charity is done in secret. Galatians 6:9–10 encourages doing good without expecting praise or reward, serving others out of genuine love, not for self-glorification.

Grace consideration: Focusing on quiet consistency rather than public affirmation. When you affirm good work without rewarding self-congratulation, you model a deeper kind of service that highlights what they often overlook: sincerity without spotlight.

It's easy to confuse activity with authenticity. But when goodness is real, it doesn't need an audience. It breathes life quietly, without needing applause.

7. Somatic Narcissist

This type builds identity through image. When they feel empty inside, they try to look full on the outside.

Description: Somatic narcissists focus on their physical appearance or bodily image, seeking admiration for their looks, fitness, or sexual appeal.

They see their physicality as a source of power and use it to draw attention and admiration from others.

Costume Details:

- Obsessed with their physical appearance or sexual desirability.
- Regularly flaunts their body to gain attention.
- May use their attractiveness or fitness to manipulate others.
- Views their body as their greatest asset and often seeks validation through it.
- May struggle with aging or physical decline, as their sense of worth is tied to their appearance.

Psychological Insights: Somatic narcissists place immense value on their external image because they equate it with their worth. This type of narcissism is often rooted in the need for external validation and fear of being "forgotten" or rejected once their physical appearance changes.

Biblical Perspective: 1 Peter 3:3–4 encourages inner beauty over outward adornment, focusing on a gentle and quiet spirit rather than physical appearance. Proverbs 31:30 teaches that beauty fades, but a woman who fears the Lord is to be praised, redirecting focus from external to internal qualities.

Grace consideration: Seeing through the surface and speaking to the soul. By refusing to measure worth through appearance, you challenge their insecurity with dignity—reminding them (and yourself) that value isn't something that fades.

8. Exhibitionist Narcissist

This type is loudest in the room—but their need for attention often hides deep insecurity.

Description: Exhibitionist narcissists crave attention and are often dramatic or theatrical in their behaviors. They seek the spotlight and will go to great lengths to ensure that they are the center of attention in any situation.

Costume Details:

- Craves constant attention and admiration.
- May exaggerate or embellish their stories or achievements.
- Can be dramatic or theatrical to draw attention to themselves.
- May engage in attention-seeking behaviors, like making controversial statements or wearing outrageous outfits.
- Has a need to be constantly noticed or validated.

Psychological Insights: Exhibitionist narcissists thrive on attention because it feeds their need for validation. They may not be comfortable with quiet or humble settings and will do anything to keep themselves in the public eye.

Biblical Perspective: Matthew 6:5–6 teaches that true acts of devotion should not be done to be seen by others but to honor God in secret. Humility is celebrated in Scriptures like Micah 6:8, which calls us to act justly, love mercy, and walk humbly with God.

Grace consideration: Allowing silence to do the heavy lifting. You don't need to compete with their drama or match their volume. Gentle presence and non-reaction often expose the emptiness behind their need for attention.

9. Victim Narcissist

This one's especially confusing for the compassionate. They don't dominate with strength—they control with suffering.

Description: Victim narcissists use their victimhood as a way to manipulate others. They constantly feel oppressed or misunderstood and use their perceived victim status to gain sympathy, attention, and control. They are easily confused with, but differ from vulnerable narcissists in core motivations, behavior patterns and emotional tactics—often more overt vs.

covert.

Costume Details:

- Frequently see themselves as a victim of circumstance or others.
- Use their victim status to manipulate others into feeling sorry for them.
- Often fails to take responsibility for their actions or circumstances.
- Can be passive-aggressive or openly hostile when their victim status is challenged.
- May use guilt or pity to control others.

Psychological Insights: The victim narcissists' focus on their own suffering prevents them from taking responsibility for their actions. They tend to feel entitled to others' support and will often play on others' empathy to avoid accountability.

Biblical Perspective: Romans 12:15 encourages believers to rejoice with those who rejoice and mourn with those who mourn, while reminding us that our ultimate hope is not in victimhood but in the hope of Christ. Colossians 3:13 teaches forgiveness, urging us not to use our past as a way to manipulate or control.

Grace consideration: Holding compassion and clarity at the same time. You can acknowledge their pain without taking on their guilt. Their story loses its grip when you stop playing the role they've assigned you.

10. Narcissistic Parent

This last type discussed here leaves wounds that echo into adulthood. It's hard to grow free when love was always conditional.

Description: Narcissistic parents often prioritize their own needs, desires, and emotional well-being over the needs of their children. They see their children as extensions of themselves and may be overly controlling or emotionally neglectful.

Costume Details:

- Expects children to meet their emotional needs or desires.
- May use children to bolster their own self-image.
- Can be neglectful of the child's true emotional needs.
- Often guilt-trips or manipulates the child for their own benefit.
- May display an idealized version of their child, forcing them into roles they don't want.

Psychological Insights: Narcissistic parents see their children as tools to further their own self-image. This leads to emotionally stunted children who may struggle with their sense of self-worth, boundary-setting, and self-esteem in adulthood.

Biblical Perspective: Ephesians 6:4 advises fathers not to exasperate their children but to bring them up in the training and instruction of the Lord. Proverbs 22:6 teaches the importance of training children with wisdom, love, and care.

Grace consideration: Honoring what's true without dishonoring yourself. As you grow into your own story, their control begins to weaken. Sometimes the most healing thing you can do is live freely—without needing their permission.

* * *

Each mask serves a purpose—even if it's only to protect a fragile heart. Seeing the mask isn't about judgment; it's about compassion with clear eyes. And in every costume, there's always the possibility of a soul ready to be free.

We've now *explored all ten patterns. While other patterns exist, you now carry a new way to understand and navigate these dynamics. Remember, the person behind narcissistic traits can remove the costume and choose instead grace, forgiveness, and love in a day of their choosing. Beneath the mask, a person worthy of love and in need of healing is waiting to be seen. And those who respond to the costume have the power to do so with healing grace.*

Appendix C: Foundational and Epistemological Disruptions

The Hidden Framework Behind This Book

In this book, disruption does not mean destruction. It means holy interruption—a pause in the patterns, mistakes, and assumptions that keep us stuck. These are not loud revolutions but quiet realignments: clarifying truths that restore emotional, relational, and spiritual integrity.

The life and ministry of Jesus were profoundly disruptive. He dismantled power structures, healed outside the expected systems, confronted both religious elitism and cultural brokenness, and redefined love as sacrificial and redemptive. Those same themes humbly echo here—not as proclamation, but as the lived experience of healing.

What follows is a brief summary of twenty-two paradigm shifts woven through this narrative. Some are only lightly referenced in the main text, yet they form the hidden framework behind the message. Together they reveal a new way to see brokenness, healing, and human transformation. For clarity, these disruptions are grouped by theme.

I. Foundational Shifts: The Structure Beneath the Message

1. Faith-Inclusive, Not Faith-Exclusive

Creates space for all readers—believers, skeptics, and seekers—without compromising truth. The door remains open wide, just as Jesus welcomed all to the table.

2. Healing Without Pressure: The Gentle Invitation to Christ

Faith is offered as a source of hope, never forced as a condition for healing—echoing how Jesus invited without coercion.

3. Psychology and Scripture: Side by Side, Not in Conflict

Shows how biblical wisdom and psychological insight work together to support healing. Truth is not afraid of evidence.

4. From the Trenches: Not the Podium

Shares from lived experience rather than clinical distance or spiritual hierarchy—inviting trust through transparency.

5. The Story Is the Message

Transformation is not taught from a distance; it is modeled in real time through personal and relational breakthroughs.

6. Compassion for Narcissists Without Excusing Harm

Offers a redemptive lens that views narcissists as both perpetrators and products of pain—affirming justice while holding space for mercy.

7. Compassion for Empaths Without Excusing Codependency

Reframes self-sacrificial behavior not as virtue, but as misdirected love—pointing to a better model rooted in identity and boundaries.

8. A Living Picture of Walking with God

Rather than prescribing beliefs or behaviors, the book reveals how a relationship with God transforms every layer of life.

9. A Reproducible Framework for Faith-Integrated Counseling

Provides a story-based model that supports emotional healing while grounded in Scripture—usable by professionals and laypeople alike.

10. The Narrow Path: A Universal Human Journey to Love and Security

Introduces a transformative model of relational decision-making that replaces false childhood binaries with biblical maturity and wholeness.

II. Strategic and Relational Clarity: Making the Invisible Visible

11. Building Discernment in the Fog of Emotion

Equips readers to identify manipulation, self-deception, and relational fog through concrete frameworks in the appendices.

12. A New Framework for Healing from Manipulation

Reveals grace, forgiveness, and love not as abstract virtues but as surgical instruments that heal even the deepest wounds.

13. Redefining Roles: Narcissists and Empaths as Trauma Mirrors

Replaces the villain/hero dichotomy with a nuanced view: both roles can emerge from unhealed pain, and both can be transformed.

14. Replacing Conditional Love with Agape Love

Contrasts worldly love (transactional, manipulative) with God's love (unconditional, redemptive), offering a new foundation for every relationship.

15. Redefining Forgiveness and Responsibility

Clarifies the difference between forgiveness and reconciliation, liberating readers from emotional burdens disguised as spiritual obedience.

III. Integrated Synergy: Disruptions That Emerge Only Together

16. The Triad of Grace, Forgiveness, and Love

These are not isolated virtues but a relational ecosystem that moves us from survival to transformation.

17. Demonstrating Truth Through Lived Experience

Rather than only describing healing, the book shows it validating biblical principles through personal, relational, and emotional fruit.

IV. Epistemological Disruptions: Rethinking What's Real

18. Scripture as the Complete Diagnosis and Design

Scripture is treated not just as wisdom but as the blueprint for human flourishing—offering what psychology alone cannot: a whole, holy map for the human condition.

19. Experience as Epistemology

Lived transformation becomes evidence that Scripture works—not courtroom proof, but the undeniable witness of fruit and testimony.

20. The Bible as Source Code: Not Just Symbol

The book does not treat the Bible as metaphor or moral guide, but as the original architecture of healing—subtle, powerful, enduring.

V. Cultural and Relational Disruptions: Shifting the Landscape

21. Healing Through Shared Humanity, Not Hierarchy

Rather than reinforcing expert-patient dynamics, the book models co-healing and shared vulnerability—like Jesus kneeling to wash feet.

22. Calling Culture Back to Relational Integrity

Individual healing ripples outward, restoring not only families and communities but also the cultural foundation of trust and truth.

Each disruption is a doorway. Together they form a map for living whole, loving well, and walking in freedom.

What begins as a holy interruption ends as quiet restoration—not just for you, but for everyone your life touches.

So even here—at the edge of the framework—our steps are not finished. Keep walking. The narrow path of grace, forgiveness, and love always leads deeper into freedom.

Final Reflections

Acknowledgments

This book would not exist without the grace of God, who has been my healer, guide, and constant source of strength. Every insight, every word of love and restoration in these pages belongs to Him.

To my family and close friends—thank you for walking beside me through both the valleys and the quiet victories. Your presence has been a refuge and a living reminder of what love can endure and become.

To those who have shared your stories of pain and resilience—whether privately or through your own work—you have given me a deeper understanding of the human heart. Your honesty and courage shaped this book more than you will ever know.

I am also grateful for the counselors, pastors, mentors, and thinkers whose wisdom has illuminated both the beauty and brokenness of our relationships. Your voices have been lighthouses on this journey, helping me find clarity in places I once could not see.

And to the readers who will hold this book with open hands and hearts—this was written for you. My hope is that within these pages you will find not only clarity, but healing, freedom, and a deeper, more enduring love.

Finally, I want to acknowledge the thoughtful use of advanced AI as a supporting tool in organizing, clarifying, and refining ideas during the writing process. Every word has been prayerfully reviewed and shaped by me to ensure it reflects my voice, lived experience, and discernment.

N. Paul Friederichs

About the Author

N. Paul Friederichs never planned to write a book. He grew up in a troubled home and carried wounds from childhood into adulthood without realizing how deeply they shaped his life. Though he pursued education, law school, and a demanding career, an inner emptiness remained. Anxiety, depression, and CPTSD became quiet companions, and even physical pain—like crippling gout—echoed the turmoil within.

A turning point began unexpectedly when a colleague handed him a copy of the ACEs study, opening a slow door to understanding trauma. That study sparked a growing curiosity about the ways early experiences shape adult behavior and relationships. Over time, Paul began to explore psychology more seriously—not as an academic, but as someone desperate to understand why the heart can feel so fragmented, even when life appears successful on the surface.

While seeking help, Paul also entered counseling, still searching for peace and clarity. One day, a counselor simply told him, "You're fine. What you really need is a closer walk with God."

Later, a friend gently helped him recall a story from his own life—a story of hope and love that had been hidden in plain sight. Paul now calls it the Pumpkin Pie story. In that moment of remembering, he felt God's love wash over him, and the weight of CPTSD lifted. Soon after, in a prayer of thanksgiving, the anxiety that had shadowed him for years vanished as if drawn out by a quiet, unseen hand. The gout, the depression—all of it—was gone. In its place came peace, joy, and a happiness he had never known before.

That experience changed everything. It led Paul into the deepest study of Scripture he had ever undertaken, while also continuing to explore psychology as a way of naming and testing what Scripture had long revealed. He began to see how the Bible speaks profoundly about the very struggles psychology describes—narcissism, empathy, broken love, and the path to restoration. By pairing biblical truth with psychological insight, he discovered a clear, grace-filled way forward that brought together everything he had been searching for: love, security, and transformation.

Beyond the Toxic Dance is the fruit of that journey. It is not written from a place of expertise or lofty credentials, but from lived experience—a fellow traveler's map toward freedom, healing, and wholeness in God.

www.ingramcontent.com/pod-product-compliance
Lightning Source LLC
LaVergne TN
LVHW022201200926
848481LV00006B/1806

* 9 7 9 8 9 9 9 6 7 4 5 1 7 *